T0059909

THE Wild HANDBOOK

A STUDIO PRESS BOOK

First published in the UK in 2021 by Studio Press Books,
an imprint of Bonnier Books UK,
4th Floor, Victoria House, Bloomsbury Square, London WC1B 4DA
Owned by Bonnier Books,
Sveavägen 56, Stockholm, Sweden

www.bonnierbooks.co.uk

© Studio Press Books, 2021
Illustrations © James Weston Lewis, 2021

3 5 7 9 10 8 6 4 2

All rights reserved
ISBN 978-17874-1-943-8

Edited by Stephanie Milton
Designed by Nia Williams
Production by Emma Kidd

A CIP catalogue for this book is available from the British Library
Printed and bound in China

THE Wild HANDBOOK

EMILY THOMAS
JAMES WESTON LEWIS

STUDIO
PRESS

CONTENTS

SUMMER

AUTUMN

INTRODUCTION

The Wild Handbook began to take shape some months into the COVID-19 pandemic. It was a time of significant change for many of us – we found ourselves confined to our homes for most of the day, allowed out only for food shopping and limited daily exercise. We couldn't meet our friends in cafés, bars or restaurants and we had to keep our distance from anyone not in our household.

But, during all this uncertainty, one thing remained the same: the natural world. Our gardens, parks, woodlands, rivers, lakes and seas were all still there for us to enjoy. With more time on our hands, many of us realised how the stresses of modern life had gradually pulled us away from the natural world, and we began to find little ways to reconnect with nature. We discovered a newfound appreciation for the beauty and healing power of the natural world – we took comfort in the early morning dawn chorus, the sound of bees buzzing and pollinating and the simple joy of eating a meal outdoors.

We've created *The Wild Handbook* to help you reconnect with nature and improve your physical and mental wellbeing in the process. It's a book you can dip in and out of when the mood strikes, or devour in one sitting. Organised by season, there are activity ideas to suit everyone, no matter your location, budget or level of fitness. From filling your home with natural décor and essential oils, learning to grow herbs and vegetables on a windowsill and spending an afternoon forest bathing, to moonbathing, walking through a snowstorm and wild swimming, you'll find plenty of ideas to suit your lifestyle.

This handbook will help you to live your very best life, in harmony with the natural world.

SPRING

EARTHING

Earthing, or 'barefoot healing' is a real thing! It's a no-lose way to boost health, and a great introduction to nature exploration. Earthing is thought to be beneficial to our physical health, and it encourages mental and emotional equilibrium, too.

After the rigours of winter, our bodies need some respite from months of going head to head with common cold and flu viruses, and working hard to keep us warm and protected against the harsher temperatures. Through our close connection to the earth, we are treating ourselves to the equivalent of a spring clean, rebooting our tired immune system for the new season.

Earthing works when we connect bare feet to earth and allow nature's electrical charge to rebalance our own atomic electricity. This is important for our immune system's defence against injury and illness, much as antioxidants are. There are myriad reasons why we can be thrown off electrical balance: too much hard exercise, cardiovascular illness or issues, winter hibernation, lapses in good diet, stress and anxiety and emotional trauma or distress. All of these life or lifestyle challenges can drain our natural battery, and require us to recharge. Earthing helps us to heal, reduces pain and inflammation, and wakes us up.

HOW TO ACHIEVE OPTIMUM EARTHING

1. Find a tranquil space outside such as a garden, park or beach. Set out early to limit social contact, but take a friend if you like. Make sure you dress for the weather, with easily removeable socks and shoes.

2. Check that the ground is safe to walk on barefoot. Try and choose areas where the grass is short, or the sand is dense, flat and smooth, and where hidden dangers, such as glass, sharp rocks or stones and any other nasties are visible and so avoidable.

3. Take off your shoes and socks, and start with some playful exploration; try running or walking barefoot across the grass or sand.

4. With your naked feet on the earth, rest one hand on the crown of your head. For 30 seconds, stand with your back straight and register the tingling in your feet. Try and empty your mind of all thoughts. Concentrate on what you're feeling and the sensations you experience. Try and stay in each second as your body communicates with the ground.

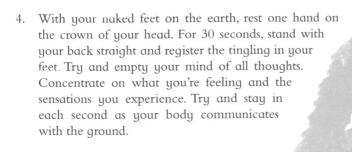

5. Stand like a tree. With your feet parallel and shoulder-width apart, keep your back straight, then place your hands in a natural position – at your sides, or resting on your stomach. Focus on your bodyweight and imagine that any tension is leaving you; visualise it sinking down to your feet and into the ground, as though it is taking root. You can hold this pose for up to 10 minutes.

6. If possible, make your Earthing a regular weekly or monthly practice.

FLING OPEN YOUR WINDOWS

The long, chilly, dark days of winter have finally come to an end. The mornings are starting to get lighter and nature is waking up. We're often a little slow and sleepy when it comes to embracing spring and it can take us a while to notice what's occurring in the world outside, but we can mark our entry into this most hopeful and delicate new season by letting some of what's outside into our homes.

1. Grab a sweater and fling open a window that offers a good view, even if that's just a couple of treetops looming overhead or a space between blocks of flats.

2. Sit or stand by the window, or safely lean out of it, and let your senses absorb the weather. Allow the breeze to touch and awaken your skin. If it's raining, shut your eyes and listen. Rain can be incredibly calming, and it is deeply nurturing for the earth; shed any negative associations with rain and concentrate on how it sounds as you think about its crucial role in nature.

3. If you have access to a garden or outdoor space, notice the colours of the grass and flowers, and what you can smell. Take in the brown leaves turning to green, the dew on the grass, perhaps some early blossom on trees, and scan for the sight of spring flowers.

4. There are things to see even if you don't have a garden or much green space nearby, and urban areas can be quite interesting in spring. Look up at the sky and you will see birds. You may also spot other wildlife or the odd fox at ground level, too. Wildlife tends to be visible early in the morning.

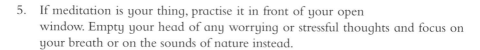

5. If meditation is your thing, practise it in front of your open window. Empty your head of any worrying or stressful thoughts and focus on your breath or on the sounds of nature instead.

Let spring soothe you for a few minutes before you go about your day.

DIGITAL DETOX

We love our devices and they're invaluable tools for modern life; they make our professional and social lives easier and give us quick access to important information. If used moderately, social media can be a great way to keep in touch with our friends, as well as keeping us informed about current affairs and news. It also gives us a platform to share our feelings and what's happening in our own lives. It can help us feel more connected and stave off loneliness, but it can be very easy to replace real life activities with incessant scrolling and tapping on our phones. Constant monitoring of what people are doing and saying, or how they look, can make us feel inadequate, unnecessarily competitive and frazzled – without us even realising it. If we overindulge, screen time can make us feel irritable and lethargic, and can wear down our sense of individuality – all before we've had breakfast! Our heads are buzzing with visual information overload, and by the end of the day we can feel drained, agitated, suffer from fuzzy vision and find ourselves unable to sleep well. It's time for a digital detox.

1. Set aside some time to eliminate the apps on your phone that you rarely use, leaving your screen uncluttered. This way, you'll only have access to the services you genuinely need.

2. Unless you absolutely need to be on call for something, make it a rule to switch off your phone or device an hour before you go to sleep. Ideally, leave it outside your bedroom, where you can't reach for it and turn it on again. Try not to switch it on in the morning until after you've had breakfast.

3. If you use your phone to check work emails, make sure you turn notifications off out of working hours and all weekend. Notifications can make us feel like we have to answer emails immediately, no matter the time of day, but we don't!

4. If you're a social-media fan, spring is a good time to ease off or give yourself a break. Work out a schedule for checking platforms like Twitter, Facebook and Instagram. Allow one hour per day, spread across the entire day. If one of your media apps tends to leave you feeling down more often than not, then consider deactivating it for a while. Your world will not fall apart as a result; most likely you'll feel lighter, calmer, more refreshed and alert, and ready to engage IRL.

COMBAT SPRING FATIGUE

In spring, we're told we should feel great because the sun is shining and new life is blooming, but we might be feeling tired, irritable, more prone to headaches and generally a bit down. This counter-intuitive response is referred to as Seasonal Affective Disorder and it's to do with our hormones adjusting to nature. During the winter months we produce more melatonin – the sleep hormone – but as the days get lighter and longer, this hormone is overlaid by another one: serotonin – the hormone that wakes us up. As our body slowly switches from melatonin to serotonin, the adjustment leaves us lethargic and tetchy. The good news is, there are ways to combat the physical and mental effects of spring fatigue. Here are some ideas.

1. Gradually increase the amount of time you spend outdoors. If you have a garden, take a drink outside and sit in nature for 20 minutes before the day begins. Turn your face up to the sky and focus on your breathing, on birdsong or on the rustle of wildlife. If you don't have outside space, grab a travel mug or flask and go for a walk. Turn your wrists up to the sun for optimum absorption of vitamin D via the delicate skin there.

2. Certain carb-laden foods release sugar too quickly, leaving us lethargic, so start the day with slow-release carbs such as porridge oats, and antioxidant fruits like blueberries. Check out spring's seasonal fruits and vegetables and make sure you're well stocked. Put almonds, cashews and Brazil nuts on your shopping list, too, as between them they contain vital vitamin E, iron, zinc, selenium and magnesium, as well as fibre. Limit sugar-rich food, but don't deprive yourself of the odd treat; you'll only crave it more! Keep yourself well hydrated throughout the day.

3. Exercise more. Take a walk in your local park or nearby countryside – somewhere hilly rather than flat is ideal. Go for a swim, a bike ride, or play badminton or tennis. Walk home with your shopping rather than driving or getting the bus. Climb those stairs instead of taking the lift. Set yourself a goal of half an hour of movement a day, and remember all movement is good. If you find it hard to motivate yourself this way, plan to exercise with a friend.

GET CREATIVE OUTSIDE

Tapping in to our creative brain doesn't require special expertise or skill. Remember how happy we felt as small children, with paints and crayons, or a pen and paper, as we created our mini-masterpieces – it was so easy to lose ourselves in the activity. But as we get older we become more self-conscious, more concerned with how well we create rather than how the act of creating makes us feel. Lots of adults simply don't bother being creative because we don't think we'll be any good.

But we're missing the point: creativity is simply expression. Expressing ourselves, whether through writing something down, playing an instrument, making something out of clay or creating a meal, is good for the soul. The joy is in the task, and once we shed our inhibitions and our need to be perfect, the feeling of wellbeing that comes with organic creativity puts us in touch with profound pleasure. Spring's colours, sights and smells provide excellent inspiration. If it's sketching you're, er, drawn to, you don't need expensive paints or pencils to create something wonderful. Whether you don a beret and sit by a tranquil river painting ducks, or take a blank notebook and a pen or pencil and spend your lunch hour on a park bench writing down the first few lines of a story, you're kick-starting your creative gene, with nature as your muse.

Don't put pressure on yourself to achieve too much too quickly. Allow yourself to sit and observe what's around you, try and empty your mind of practical or anxious thoughts and everyday obstacles. Instead, focus on how you feel. Are you drawn to something in particular? Start slowly and either sketch it with a pencil or jot down your thoughts. If you're keen to write creatively, sit and allow inspiration to come for the first line of your book.

Don't judge what you've done with negativity. Resist scoring yourself or throwing away your work in a fit of frustration. If your mind goes blank, let it. Getting annoyed with yourself only reverses the positive effects of endeavour. Give yourself permission to pause, put your work in progress away and return to it with a clear head another time.

THE POWER OF BLUE

Walking through a bluebell wood is widely believed to
reduce our levels of cortisol – the stress hormone – as well
as boost the immune system. And the colour of bluebells
contains its own special superpower, as blue is a naturally
soothing and stress-busting colour.

Bluebell woods can be found everywhere, so you likely
won't have to travel far to find one. In Britain, there is a small
window of time for you to see bluebells, ranging from early February to the end
of March, depending on how long and cold the winter has been. A mild February
will see bluebells flower and vanish early, while an extended cold snap means they
will come up later. Keep an eye on the weather, and be prepared for a spontaneous
bluebell-wood dash!

DAFFODIL LOVE

The Common Daffodil, also known as the Trumpet Narcissus, is common in
Northern Europe, but grows anywhere in the world with a cooler climate. Often a
vivid yellow, daffodils are the classic symbol of spring. Author A.A. Milne referred
to them as 'sun bonnets' and poet William Wordsworth was so convinced of their
uplifting power that he wrote a poem, 'I Wandered Lonely as a Cloud', in homage to
them. If you visit Britain's Lake District in spring, you'll see why he was so inspired
– in this region they are glorious and abundant. Daffodils can also be white (with
contrasting yellow inner petals), pink and even orange. Stop and take notice of these
beauties; they are often taken for granted as they are so common. Make it a mission
to seek out the different varieties, photograph them and add them to your Instagram
spring journal. You can grow your own, too, and they will even thrive on an indoor
window ledge if you don't have a garden. Plant bulbs in the autumn, and watch
them bloom in late winter or early spring. Be careful not to touch the inner petals
too much, though, as they can cause an allergic reaction.

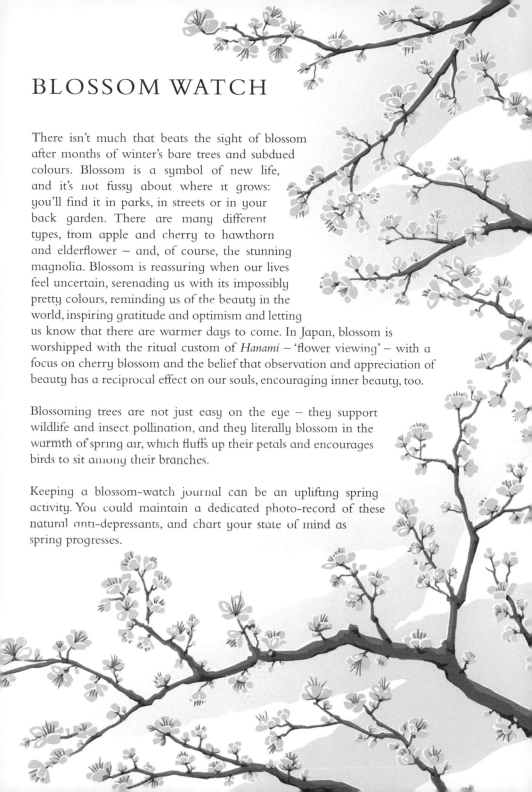

BLOSSOM WATCH

There isn't much that beats the sight of blossom after months of winter's bare trees and subdued colours. Blossom is a symbol of new life, and it's not fussy about where it grows: you'll find it in parks, in streets or in your back garden. There are many different types, from apple and cherry to hawthorn and elderflower — and, of course, the stunning magnolia. Blossom is reassuring when our lives feel uncertain, serenading us with its impossibly pretty colours, reminding us of the beauty in the world, inspiring gratitude and optimism and letting us know that there are warmer days to come. In Japan, blossom is worshipped with the ritual custom of *Hanami* – 'flower viewing' – with a focus on cherry blossom and the belief that observation and appreciation of beauty has a reciprocal effect on our souls, encouraging inner beauty, too.

Blossoming trees are not just easy on the eye — they support wildlife and insect pollination, and they literally blossom in the warmth of spring air, which fluffs up their petals and encourages birds to sit among their branches.

Keeping a blossom-watch journal can be an uplifting spring activity. You could maintain a dedicated photo-record of these natural anti-depressants, and chart your state of mind as spring progresses.

BIRD SPOTTING

Spring is the time to reboot your brain after months of the harshest season; during winter we tend to focus on keeping warm, and perhaps over-indulge in food and alcohol as a way to cope with the darker skies, shorter days and winter viruses. We can emerge tired and emotionally low. No wonder we start dreaming of holidays abroad, or spa breaks at this time of year. What many of us overlook is that there is a natural remedy to the winter blues that centres on what's above and around us: bird-watching. Engaging with these incredible creatures encourages gratitude, calm and perspective as we marvel at their colours, physicality and sounds. Bird-watching is not a mysterious art, nor does it require dressing in an anorak and hiding in a shrub for hours with a pair of binoculars. All you really need are your eyes and a little preparation beforehand, so you know how to recognise different species.

HOW TO PREPARE FOR BIRD-WATCHING

1. Do a little research into the birds that will be in season where you live. The birds that gather in urban areas will be different to those gathering in rural areas, and different birds come and go at different times of the day, as well as throughout the year. Make a list of the birds you want to look out for, including size and colouring, and take this with you so you can refer to it.

2. Check a weather app before you head out, so you can make sure you're properly dressed. Always wear comfortable, enduring footwear. Layering your clothes is never a bad idea, nor is having a pair of gloves, a waterproof jacket and sunscreen in your backpack.

3. Pack a rucksack with some handy bird-watching tools: binoculars and a field guide will help optimise your experience. A camera is a good idea, though if you have a smart phone, that will suffice. You'll need a portable charger for your devices, and some snacks and drink to keep you fuelled and hydrated.

If you're lucky and manage to take some decent photos, you can create a bird album. If you commit to bird-watching, it won't be long before you're impressing your friends with your knowledge and noticing how good it makes you feel.

MAKE A BIRD FEEDER

Unsurprisingly, birds' natural food supply is harder to come by in the colder months of winter and spring, but it's a good idea to help out our feathered friends all year round by setting up a bird feeder in your garden or on a decent-sized window ledge. You can buy them, but it's much more satisfying to make your own. If you know what you're doing, you can adapt your feeding stations to attract different kinds of birds. Modern farming methods and an increase in tidy gardens (and so a decrease in wild gardens) mean that we see fewer birds such as finches, buntings or sparrows as they are not drawn to these unnatural spaces. Sunflower seeds are safe for all of these species, but do your research on the best food for different birds. Be patient, and wait for wary birds to discover your food source. Once they realise you're friendly, they'll start visiting regularly. Feel the glow of taking care of precious wildlife!

MAKING YOUR BIRD TABLE

1. You'll need some basic tools to put your table together: nails, hooks, a hammer and some sandpaper. Seek expert advice if you're new to woodwork.

2. Buy some solid and sustainable wood that won't crack or get damaged by the rain or harsher weather. Seek advice from a timber merchant, if you can. Ideally the wood should be between half a centimetre and a centimetre in thickness.

3. Try to make your table as big as possible, to avoid a posse of birds competing with each other for food and putting off the more timid varieties.

4. To keep the food safely on your table, create a rim about one centimetre high around the edge, leaving corner gaps so that rain can drain away. This will also make cleaning the table easier.

5. Before you put your feeder table together, sand down the wood to remove cracks and crevices that could harbour dirt, leading to disease or infection. It's not advisable to treat or varnish the wood, but, if you must, then use a water-based treatment and be sure it is completely dry before the table is used.

6. Add some nails or hooks on the side of the table to hang a bags of nuts and seeds from. You could also make a roof for your table, which provides protection from predatory birds such as hunting sparrowhawks, and keeps the food dry.

SPRING SCAVENGER HUNT

Scavenger hunts aren't just for kids: this fun activity helps to put us all in touch with nature. We can feel the stresses of life fade away, replaced by the delight of identifying seasonal wildlife, plants and flowers in both urban and rural areas. With the bounty of new life appearing around us, spring is a great time to embark on a scavenger hunt, but you can make them a seasonal event. To prepare, simply research the items you might find; it will be all the more satisfying if you know beforehand which seasonal items you're looking for. Put together a checklist and take it with you, bearing in mind that your list will vary depending on where you live. If you're feeling particularly ambitious, you could turn your scavenger hunt into a mini-break. If you live in a big city, you could take a trip somewhere with a dramatically different landscape and combine it with a staycation.

Learn how to spot a chiffchaff, a tree bee, some dog willow or wild garlic. Open your eyes to the world around you, and give your busy, buzzing brain something supremely soothing and satisfying to focus on. You can collect souvenirs of your scavenge, too. Leaves and branches, flowers (though check you can pick them first) and treefall, and then turn to pages 24–25 and 44 to learn how to craft these items into beautiful spring décor for your home.

1. First, decide where you're going to go on your spring hunt. If you're a city or town dweller with limited funds, keep it local. If you are able to travel, make sure you research how crowded your chosen destination might be. If you're not keen on encountering hordes of kids on their school holidays, then plan your scavenger hunt during term time.

2. Check out weather conditions and temperatures in your chosen area, as well as what sort of terrain you'll encounter, then dress accordingly. Pack a bag with a phone charger, some food and drink, gloves and binoculars if you can get hold of them – and something foldable and portable to safely keep your finds in.

3. Once you've researched the nature and wildlife that's native to your chosen destination, make a note of how to recognise it. Try to include as much detail as you can: distinct colours, shapes, markings, smells and sounds. Everyone knows what badgers look like, but goat willow is perhaps not quite so familiar.

4. Be respectful of nature. Don't go barging into an area, upsetting wildlife and trampling over plants. Be gentle and cautious. Most wild animals in the UK won't hurt you, but they might be frightened of you, so tread carefully around them. And some plants and flowers may be harmful if you touch them. Make a note of things to be wary or protective of and handle with care!

MAKE A SPRING WREATH

The colours and smells of spring are evidence of nature getting ready to bloom and begin its cycle again, and they can bring such pleasure. Spring marks the end of the harsher winter months and signals optimism, as we look forward to peeling off the layers and immersing ourselves in the great outdoors again. One way to keep in touch with nature at this time of year is by keeping a little of it in our homes. Making a spring wreath to hang on a door or wall is a great way to combine nature with creativity. We can combine the treasures we find outside – wood, leaves and flowers – to make a glorious spring halo, reminding us what this incredible season has to offer and how instantly it lifts our mood.

The great thing about making your own wreath is that you are crafting something unique: selecting your favourite forages from outside and weaving them together to suit your own style. Some people like ornate, showy wreaths with burlap ribbons; others prefer wilder, more natural-looking rings. Whatever your style, you can create a wreath to suit you, and bring a little spring joy to your friends and family, too.

Since there are many different methods for this craft, there are also many online tutorials to choose from. You'll be able to find one that suits your location and the kinds of things you might find nearby, as well as what sort of accessories you can use. The willow-wreath guide opposite is just one idea. You can substitute twigs, vines or other natural materials for the willow – you just need to make sure that the wood is supple enough to bend when you start making your hoop. Dogwood and beech are naturally supple, but you can also use roots or vines such as grapevine, ivy or clematis.

WEAVING YOUR SPRING WILLOW WREATH

1. You'll need a pair of secateurs for cutting your willow, flowers and leaves.

2. Source your willow – you're going to need around ten to twelve whips (branches). You can cut from a weeping or standard willow tree, but if the wood is dry, you'll need to hydrate it by soaking it for a few hours, so that it doesn't crack or split when you start making your wreath base.

3. Strip the leaves from your willow stems – the stems should be around one to one and a half metres in length.

4. Your willow stems will be different sizes – some will be fatter than others. Start your weave with the skinnier ones and then add in the thicker stems.

5. Start to weave your stems together to make a hoop in your desired size. With your first stem, make sure to leave at least six inches sticking out for wrapping to the hoop with twine or wire to hold it in place.

6. Keep turning and shaping your willow stems around each other. It won't be long before the stems weave flexibly together to create a sturdy hoop.

7. If you're adding flowers, keep your willow hoop to three or four stems woven together so that you have room to incorporate the flowers. Tuck in and snip any willow stems that are sticking out, securing your hoop.

8. Now forage for your spring leaves and flowers. Hardier roses, daffodils, forsythia and lavender are good for decoration. Flowers with stronger stems are best.

9. You will need your secateurs to cut flowers and foliage, but keep the stems on all leaves and flowers as long as possible to help you insert them between your willow. Cut off any brown or wilting foliage.

10. Position your spring halo wherever you want it in your home. And remember, you can change your flowers when they wilt, and reuse your willow wreath hoop by drying it out.

VISIT A PUBLIC GARDEN

Spending time in a garden, whether it belongs to you or not, is known to lift the mood, decrease anxiety and improve physical and mental health. For one thing, increasing your exposure to vitamin D is vital for storing calcium, which you need for your bones and for strengthening your immune system. Nature really is an organic anti-depressant. At times of abnormal stress, such as the global COVID-19 pandemic, many people reported that spending time in beautiful outside spaces (when access was permitted) significantly boosted their mood and proved an invaluable coping strategy. One survey found that even just standing on a balcony could significantly decrease levels of stress and ward off depression.

Public gardens are very often attached to a big house like a grand stately home or a palace, and they can be found all over the world. In the UK, visitors can enjoy the spectacular grounds of Lyme Park in Cheshire (often used for filming period dramas), Hampton Court (King Henry VIII's home) in Kingston-upon-Thames or the majestic Chatsworth House in Derbyshire. There are many National Trust and English Heritage houses in Britain whose gardens are open to the public throughout the year, giving you the opportunity to spend a day marvelling at the extraordinary flowerbeds, trees and topiary. You might feel you've gone back in time as you stroll around acres of land, with no modern buildings or vehicles in sight. It's a wonderful way to experience the simplicity of, and the skill required to maintain a beautiful public or botanical garden.

Wherever you live you will find gardens to visit. You can find out online what times of year the gardens are open and the best times to visit them, as well as which are free to visit and which require donations or entry fees. There's something for everyone; public gardens are there for all to enjoy.

VIRTUAL GARDENS

If you're not able to go out much, or at all, you can now enjoy a virtual garden or gardening experience! Virtual garden tours became very popular when people were stuck at home during 2020's various lockdowns, offering a state-of-the-art view of nature, bringing the sights and sounds of the garden into many people's homes, and often inspiring a new appreciation for horticulture. There are also virtual gardening courses to be found online, which offer practical, step-by-step lessons on how to design and plant your own garden.

FOREST BATHING

In Japan, they call it *Shinrin-yoku*: 'forest bath'. For decades, the Japanese have considered forest bathing a vital part of preventative healthcare: good for body and soul. Japanese doctors endorse the practice, not only as a stress-relieving antidote to the physical and mental toll of a busy, pressured lifestyle, but as a bona fide weapon against illnesses such as heart disease and cancer. Western doctors are getting on board, too. There is no downside to this activity!

Forest bathing does not mean actual bathing, nor does it involve water. It is the immersion of all five of our senses in the forest experience. Spending time under a leafy canopy, inhaling the unpolluted air, absorbing the sounds and smells, is a good enough mood-booster in and of itself, but the real secret lies in phytoncides. These chemicals are released by plants and trees, and are found to greatly boost the immune system and our levels of serotonin (our stress-combatting hormone).

There is some commitment required with forest bathing. Half an hour spent walking through trees won't really give you the full benefit, and in Japan, people can spend up to three days in a forest. You don't need to spend that long, but try to make time for a whole morning or afternoon in the forest or woody park of your choice.

YOUR FOREST THERAPY

1. Ideally, choose a day with dry weather. The fresh, cool air of spring is perfect as it makes it easy to breathe and move. Dress accordingly; feeling too hot or too cold may hamper your enjoyment.

2. Switch off your devices when you arrive at your destination. Without the distraction of a camera or a phone, you can devote yourself fully to being in the moment. If you are going with a friend, agree not to talk until you leave.

3. Allow yourself to explore the space at a walk, taking in the sights and sounds around you. Trust your mind and body to take you where they want to go.

4. Observe the detail of the trees and plants, and nature's extraordinary designs. Notice how your body moves and how the ground feels beneath your feet.

5. Find somewhere comfortable and dry to sit or lie down, and listen closely to the sounds all around you. Birds and other wildlife surround you, and they are sensitive to your presence. Be respectful towards them – notice how they respond to you, and how their behaviour might change as they adapt to you.

6. In this atmosphere of tranquility, focus only on what is happening in the moment. We are too used to thinking ahead and letting our thoughts spiral. By not allowing ourselves to project or plan, we are giving our minds a rest.

WINDOW LEDGE HERBS, FLOWERS AND VEG

There is little to beat the satisfaction of growing herbs, vegetables and flowers yourself. From cress and tomatoes to geraniums and hyacinths, growing stuff on our window ledge is a wonderful way to create a sense of achievement and agency when we might be feeling powerless, as well as keeping us in touch with the natural world. Sprinkling your own parsley on an omelette or tucking in to a plate of mozzarella with those small, tasty tomatoes you picked from your window box can bring great pleasure.

If you have your own outdoor space, you're one of the lucky ones. If not, congratulate yourself on your resourcefulness: you're about to take a small space and turn it into a garden. Planting and cultivating from seeds or bulbs is always possible, even if you have limited outdoor space. All you need is enough room for decent-sized containers, sunlight, water, compost, small rocks or stones, and some plant food. And spring is the time to start planting. Home growing does not initially require special containers; you can plant seeds in empty egg boxes, or yoghurt pots, or use folded cardboard toilet rolls as a biodegradable, sustainable solution before moving to bigger pots. Though you can start a seed off indoors, most need sunlight, so exposing them to daylight is important.

THE PREP

1. Do a little research to find out what you can
    realistically grow in your window box. Herbs and flowers
    are pretty straightforward, but vegetables need more thought.
    Carrots, pea-shoots and tomatoes are all suitable for window
    ledges. Other larger veg such as courgettes and potatoes
    need more room, so they won't work. You can grow beans,
    but you'll need to provide a pole to support them.

2. If you'll mostly be growing herbs and flowers, you won't need huge
    pots, but make sure they are heavy or weighted down enough so that they won't
    be blown off by a strong wind. Consider also how much weight your ledge can
    withstand. If you live high up, consider your downstairs neighbours, too. Your
    local garden centre will give you good advice on growing herbs and flowers,
    and you can buy seeds online, in garden centres and in some supermarkets.

3. Assess the conditions of your outdoor space. When and how often does it get
    the sun? Is it exposed to the elements or overshadowed by other buildings? The
    plants you choose need to be able to survive in your particular conditions. You
    can research this online, but the good news is that most herbs and plants such as
    lavender are hardy and easy to nurture.

4. For good quantities of vegetables, choose the deepest pots you can for the size
    of your windowsill. They will need to be a minimum of 15 cm deep, but ideally
    20 or even 30 cm. You can improvise by using a large tin or a non-plastic
    household container. Choosing different types of containers for different seeds
    will help you tell your sprouting veg apart, too.

5. You'll need compost that's designed for your pot – one that will hold water
    better and contains vital nutrients for growth. Consult with online or garden
    centre experts to source this, but loam-based compost is ideal.

6. Put a layer of stones in the base of your pot for water to drain through, then
    add the compost, patting it down firmly. Now you can add water: just enough
    to make the compost moist.

7. Water and feed your plants. Water often, but don't go crazy and drown your
    budding veg. To check moisture levels, put a finger down just beneath the surface
    of the compost – it should feel slightly moist, but not wet. For feeding, buy a
    liquid food and add at least once every two weeks.

WILDFLOWER FOOD FORAGE

Many wild plants and flowers are edible and can be used in cooking, and spring is the perfect season to start looking for them. You can discover the full list of items that can be found in spring by researching online, but here a few suggestions to kick things off.

Earlier in spring, you'll find chickweed: one of nature's tasty secrets, which is packed with vitamins and minerals and is delicious in salads. The dandelion (*dent de lion* – or 'lion's tooth') is a versatile flower and every part of it can be used in cooking. Its unopened buds can even be put into sauces to give a tang, much like a caper does. Gorse, often found on clifftops, is famous for its coconut and almond tasting flowers. And Japanese knotweed – a notorious problem for horticulturists – is vitamin rich. You'll be doing gardeners a favour by picking and eating it, too, so knock yourself out. In mid-spring, alexanders, a.k.a 'horse parsley', is known for its succulent stem, flowers and leaf tips and can be taken home and steamed to serve as an edible garnish. And bramble leaves are great for making tea.

You'll need to do your homework, as it's essential that you correctly identify the plants and don't mistake them for anything inedible. Edible wildflowers can be found throughout the year, so make a note of what you can find in each season and where in the country it grows. If you're an urban dweller, check out your nearest wood or green space (not your local park). Depending on what you're looking for, you may have to broaden your area. If you can afford to and have the time, hop on a train or drive further afield.

WHAT YOU NEED FOR WILDFLOWER FOOD FORAGING

1. A cotton or linen bag (a tote is ideal) for transporting your wildflowers without suffocating them. You can also take a lined basket.

2. Ideally, you should invest in an eyeglass to help you properly identify your wildflowers. Some flowers look very similar to others, so it's vital that you correctly identify them. You'll need to check the characteristics of your edible plant are exactly right to make sure you know which plants are edible and which must be avoided in case they're dangerous to consume. You can buy inexpensive eyeglasses, but if you haven't got the budget and if you're in any doubt about a plant, then just don't pick it.

3. Hardy work or gardening gloves (easily found in hardware shops or online) are a good idea, to protect your hands as you forage. Your skin may be sensitive and you could be allergic to some wildflowers.

4. A pair of pruners or secateurs for careful cutting of your wildflowers.

5. Sensible clothes. If you're immersing yourself in wildflowers, don't wear shorts — nettle rash is not much fun…

THE SEA, THE SEA!

It's no secret that spending time by the water has a marked effect on how we feel. As with stargazing (see pages 130-131), psychological studies show that an expanse of water such as a river or the sea reminds us that we are part of a vast, natural world. Focusing on our connection to this world, rather than our individual anxieties and concerns, helps to give us persepctive. We rememember that what matters is good health, good relationships and community living. This doesn't mean that our worries are insignificant or should be dismissed, but their burden can be alleviated somewhat when we open our eyes to the bigger picture.

It isn't just the sight of water that soothes us and brings us back into the moment; it's the sounds and smells, the wildlife that flocks to it, too. The Victorians often sent those recuperating from illness to the sea to complete their recovery. It's easy to see why time spent near water helps maintain and restore good mental and physical health. We arrive home tired, but in the best possible way – our bodies and minds grateful for this valuable time away from hectic modern life.

If you live in a city, you can still benefit from water therapy. If you are able to, hop on a train for a day trip to the seaside, or head to a lake or river. If not, many city parks also have great ponds and lakes. Technology can also be your friend – download an app and listen to the sounds of water. This can be particularly useful when you're experiencing a hectic time at work or in your personal life. Spend half an hour with your headphones on, and your blood-pressure will lower, your mind and body will feel calmer, and you'll feel stronger and better able to cope with stress. Trials showed that levels of stress and loneliness decreased in the elderly when they were shown videos of seas and oceans, so finding a 'sea fix' on YouTube can be hugely therapeutic, too.

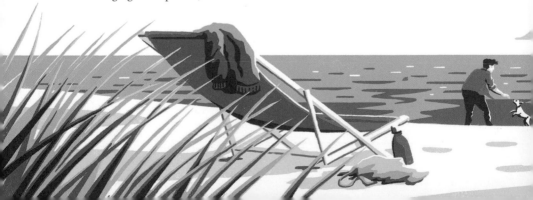

HOW TO PREPARE FOR YOUR 'WATER THERAPY'

1. Consult a reliable weather app ahead of your trip, to make sure that your experience won't include a howling gale, torrential rain, a spring hail storm, or a snow shower. That said, a bit of a breeze and some light rain can add to the exhilaration of the experience.

2. Dress for the weather. Take a light rucksack and pack a waterproof jacket, some gloves and a spare pair of socks. Depending on where you're headed, take wellies or hiking boots in case you encounter mud. Layers are a good idea; in spring, the temperature can switch from mild to chilly within a few hours, and if you're next to the sea, it will be cooler than in the city.

3. If you're going to the coast, you'll probably be able to buy snacks there, but if you're heading somewhere more remote (a mountain lake, for example), you'll need to pack some energy-giving food. Always take water with you, and check out the area's amenities beforehand so you can plan for a refill.

4. Educate yourself about the conditions in your chosen destination: find out if there are strong currents or swampy land. If you're going to the sea and you're not a strong swimmer, keep away from any areas of water marked as dangerous. If you're determined to get on or in the water, then this is particularly important – there is no shame in a life-jacket, even if you're planning a simple pedalo on a park pond.

CYCLE AWAY THE COBWEBS

By now, we know that regular exercise is not only good for our bodies, helping to reduce the likelihood of illness and disease and prevent obesity, it is good for our mental health, too. Those glorious endorphins that are released after half an hour of moderate cardio-vascular exercise significantly reduce our levels of stress and anxiety. Exercise also sharpens our brains, improving our memory and creative thinking. Then there's the rush of having challenged yourself a little physically, pushing yourself out of your comfort zone and lethargy to feel more energised. It's fun, too! Participating in team exercise, even with just one or two other people, is motivational, producing a sense of responsibility and shared experience. We're more likely to follow through with group exercise plans even when we don't feel like it – we don't want to let people down. Afterwards, we feel more bonded to others, more part of a community and ultimately fitter and more physically confident.

Committing to an expensive gym membership can be an effective way for some people to motivate themselves, but exercising outside is widely believed to be the healthiest choice as it boosts vitamin D levels and gives you the opportunity to breathe clean, fresh air. Outdoor exercise is often cheaper, too; running and wild swimming are free, as is cycling, once you've invested in a good bike. Cycling can even save you money; it can be a great alternative to public transport. Recent studies have shown that people who cycle every day experience more prolonged daily contentment compared to those who don't. Although pretty much all exercise is good, a bike is low-impact as it's easier on our joints, bones and hearts. If you're already a super cyclist then you're all set, but if the experience is new to you, here are some key tips to get you started.

1. Choose a bike that's right for your level of experience. For beginners, lightweight bikes with thinner tyres are best for road riding.

2. Get the right size bike. To test this, straddle the top tube of the bike and aim for about an inch gap between your body and the frame. If you're not sure, ask advice from bike-shop experts.

3. Consider your budget and your cycling ambitions. Will you only be using your bike for gentle rides at weekends? Is it for more strenuous exercise? Are you planning to build up to a long-distance ride? Will the terrain you ride on be smooth or hilly? Again, talk to an expert who can advise you on the right model for you, taking into account your gender, your build and your level of fitness. There are lots of different types of bikes, so take your time to choose the one that's right for you.

4. Don't forget your helmet! This is particularly important for urban cycling, but you should wear one in remote, rural areas, too.

5. Use your bike in a way that feels comfortable and realistic for you. As with every activity in this book, cycling should be fun, rewarding and stress-reducing, not stress-inducing!

CHASE THE BIRD CHORUS

We've been exposed to birdsong all our lives, but many of us haven't taken the time to properly listen to it, or to learn why birds sing and what each individual song can tell us about their habits and needs. Birdsong isn't just wonderful to hear, there's a purpose to it. It's a vital form of communication between the bird community.

Take the male warbler, which sets off from Africa for England at the start of spring, flying over 2000 miles with romance on his mind. The warbler's colouring means he blends in too well with the landscape, but he needs to stand out to attract a female, so uses his seductive voice to make himself known and get the girl. Birdsong is not just for wooing, though. It's vital in staking out territory; the bird equivalent of flexing muscles and warning other male birds off its patch.

Although all birds 'sing', only certain species are technically songbirds, meaning they practice and perfect their songs. Starlings and goldfinches, for example, love a good old sing-along together. The sounds of other birds are innate from birth and often designed for a primal purpose – like the male and female robin, who sing throughout the winter expressly to defend their territory.

Learning to identify birdsong is a hugely rewarding activity. It can help us to develop patience and learn to be silent. It can also help us to feel more connected to these extraordinary creatures and with nature in general. We are humbled by the ingenuity of wildlife, learning to stop and look outwards at the world around us for a while – a significant marker of good mental health.

BIRDSONG TIPS

1. Start with the songbirds, which in northern Europe include chaffinches, blackbirds, robins and skylarks. Each of these birds has a distinct sound, or 'tune' – songbirds make the most melodic sounds.

2. Visit a variety of locations to expose yourself to a variety of birdsong. If you're by a river or lake, here is where you'll see and hear the kingfisher or the wagtail. If you follow the sound you might even catch the vivid blue of the kingfisher's livery. If you're in a rural area with plenty of fields, then you're likely to hear the rise and fall of the skylark's call.

3. It might sound daft, but a good way of remembering individual birdsong is to apply your own words or lyrics to each – try it with the wood pigeon's four-note warble.

4. Handily, certain birds are named after their songs – the cuckoo ('cuck-oo') for instance, or the 'chiff-chaff' of the chiffchaff. Keep this in mind as you listen and it might help you identify some of the birds.

5. Birds are incredibly clever, so be aware that sometimes they mimick each other's songs. As you build on your knowledge, you'll learn to identify the fakes.

6. Believe it or not, birds have different accents depending on which country they're in, so wherever you are in the world, make sure you listen out for local sounds.

GET INVOLVED IN ALLOTMENTS

Many people consider allotment management to be a quaint, old-fashioned hobby. The fact is, renting allotment space is more popular than ever, and not just for the older generation. Those with stressful jobs, who might spend up to 12 hours a day staring at a computer screen, may find blissful release in digging their hands into soil, nurturing plants and seeds to fruition. For those of us without our own garden, connecting with nature through an allotment reaps many benefits. The simplicity of this endeavour – working in the fresh air to cultivate new life and watch nature do its thing – works wonders in decreasing our stress levels. It increases our serotonin levels, and ultimately improves our cognitive mental health, including our memory. And it's never too soon to start your allotment life. . .

Allotments are available globally. They are mostly state-owned, so the public can obtain space by applying to their local council or municipality. In the UK, that means contacting either your local parish or district council, or the National Trust, who also have spaces. They can provide you with a list of local sites, then you can add your name to the list of applicants. This can take time, as allotments are popular and waiting lists can be long, but using your newfound powers of patience, sit tight until your name comes up. You can also join forces with a group of five or six like-minded people, which will promote your application.

If the wait becomes too frustrating, it's always worth scouting out your local neighbourhood to see if there is any vacant land. Find out who owns it, then contact them to ask if you can rent the land from them. Land often sits unutilized for years and landowners might be grateful for the income!

AWESOME AWE WALKS

No, this is not just a term for a really good stomp through the park or countryside. An 'awe walk' is all about harnessing our awe of the natural world – its colours, sights and sounds – which in turn causes us to shift our mental focus outwards rather than inwards, thus lowering stress, anxiety and blood pressure. The awe walk movement has been around since the early noughties, and is more vital than ever for keeping our minds and bodies healthy.

The key is to seek out a wide, open space that's also brand new to you – a mountain with a panoramic view, for instance, or the top of a skyscraper or tall building (where permissible) in urban areas. The feeling of awe will come more naturally when it's inspired by sights and sounds that are unfamiliar to you, and it takes only a 15-minute walk to feel the benefits.

TIPS TO ACHIEVE ULTIMATE AWE

1. Turn off your devices, or leave them at home.

2. Before you set off, sit quietly or meditate to get yourself into a receptive state of mind. Avoid activity that stresses you and embrace behaviour that soothes you.

3. Turn to pages 12-13 for some tips on how to focus on your physical connection with the ground. Use this technique as you walk.

4. As you move, notice those moments that bring you awe and make your hairs stand on end: a sudden glimpse of wildlife such as a baby rabbit frolicking, or a squirrel making its mad dash up a tree, or the colour of the grass and how the ground feels beneath your feet: the beauty of nature's architecture. You'll feel your body respond to your sense of wonder, and it's the best feeling in the world.

HULA HULA!

Remember when you spent hours hula hooping as a child? Never-ending fun, right? And when you managed to get your hoop spinning around your waist for a whole minute without it dropping to the ground – how great was that?

You may have thought your hula-hooping days were over, but the good news is they're back! Not only is this activity excellent for fitness and toning, it's great for your mental health, too.

Hooping gets your heart rate up, burns calories, improves balance and coordination and harnesses the power of core mental-health stabilisers – mindfulness and meditation – which are known to reduce stress and combat depression. Hooping athletes know they are practising a mind-body-spirit sport that compels them to stay in the moment, with their focus only on keeping the hoop spinning – they call it a mindful, movement meditation. Best of all, hooping is fun, and is a worthwhile activity, even if the hoop ends up on the ground more often than not. You don't need to be good at hula hooping, just practising it is enough to reap its many benefits.

WHAT TO KNOW BEFORE HOOPING

1. As with all exercise, if you have any underlying health conditions, including problems with your heart, breathing, back or hips, it's best to check with your doctor or a physiotherapist before you embark on hooping.

2. Although hooping can be done inside if you've got enough space and are unable to leave your house, it's best done outdoors in your garden, local park or even a deserted tennis court.

3. There are different kinds of hoops, so do some research before you buy, and make sure that your hoop stretches from the tips of your toes to around your belly button when you're standing.

4. It's a good idea to check out online video tutorials first, to be sure of the technique you'll need to use as a beginner. Online videos are also a great way to check out the kind of super-hooping you can progress to.

5. It's best to wear comfortable, flexible clothing while hooping. Leggings or sweatpants are ideal, along with a T-shirt, trainers or plimsols. If you're hooping outside, make sure you wear warmer clothing, but remember that you'll heat up as you hoop. An easily removable hoodie or sweatshirt is a good idea.

6. Now prepare your playlist, plug in your headphones and you're good to go!

SPRING BRANCH DÉCOR

The simplest way to spruce up your home for spring is to use outdoor finds to decorate rooms, fireplaces, mantelpieces and doorways, and to make natural table decorations. It isn't just about the sight of spring twigs, branches, buds and leaves around you, the smell of nature will also reinvigorate your home and awaken your senses.

All you'll need is a bag or sack big enough to store your foraged finds, a pair of wellies in case you encounter any mud, and a pair of work gloves (you'll find these in hardware stores or any big supermarket). Head for your nearest patch of dense trees, and you'll find lots of fallen branches and twigs. Remember, don't break anything directly off the trees: only use materials that have already fallen. You can also keep an eye out for ivy or trailing thick-stemmed plants; you can add these to your branch décor for a snap of colour. A bit of cherry blossom décor in your bedroom will bring immediate joy.

Some hardcore spring decorators use bigger branches as curtain poles, creating a tree-house effect in their homes. If you're not quite at this level yet, you can just add a few simple touches: collect twigs and place them together in a vase for your table or mantelpiece or trail ivy over the back of a chest of drawers. For variety, spray your branches silver or a pale blue or yellow. You could make a twig nest for your jewellery, too. Make sure you clean all your wood before using it so that you don't bring any creatures inside.

There are endless ideas when it comes to decorating with natural materials – get online to find more inspiration.

SPRING PHOTOSHOOT

Keep a written journal of your outdoor spring experience, and take photos to illustrate it. Begin with your emergence from winter, noting the feelings and thoughts you have during the transition, and chart how your moods change as you explore nature. You could even set up a Facebook or Instagram account devoted to your spring diary, so others can share your experience. If you started the season a little fatigued or low in mood, record this and accompany it with a visual – the view out of your window, perhaps, as a first step to spring healing. You can keep your journal private and just for yourself, but studies show that by expressing your feelings and sharing them with others, along with any activities you've found to lift your mood and improve your mental health, you're engaging with those who empathise and identify with you. This combats loneliness – yours and other people's – and is inspiring and motivational. Remember that it's OK to not be OK. Later, when your mood is up and your anxiety is reduced, you'll be cheered on by a community of like-minded humans.

SUMMER

WILD SWIMMING

More and more of us are discovering the joys of wild swimming. If you're new to the concept, wild swimming is not jumping into your local leisure-centre pool and thrashing about in an uncontrolled manner. Wild swimming is simply swimming outside in a natural (not man-made) stretch of salt or fresh water, be that a river, a lake or the open sea. Back in the day, folk might have called it just 'swimming', but here in the 21st century, with our easy access to modern, manufactured pools, jumping into unchlorinated, cold water can feel pretty wild.

Since we're used to heated indoor and outdoor pools, it can be daunting to consider immersing ourselves in chilly, unknown waters – and if you can't swim, you must not try this activity. But if you're game, the benefits are well worth it. Not only does wild swimming stimulate muscle function and vasodilation (healthy blood-flow), it has been cited by athletes as a vital part of their pre-performance training, so it makes a great warm-up before a jog or a run.

The effects aren't just physical, either. The positive effect of a cold dip on our mental health is also significant. Wild swimming quickly triggers endorphins in our nervous system, creating a feeling of euphoria, where all our senses come alive. It takes a little bit of courage to take the plunge and, as with overcoming a challenge of any size, feeling the fear and doing it anyway is unbeatable when it comes to building mental strength and confidence. Wild swimming relieves stress and encourages an in-the-moment state, when we allow ourselves to experience bodily sensations and remain largely free of other thoughts.

HOW TO PREPARE FOR YOUR WILD SWIM

1. Seek out a stretch of water that matches your swimming skill in terms of the nature of the water. You should also consider any sea or pond life you may encounter; if you're sea swimming, there's a chance you might feel fish swimming around you and, in many rivers, reeds and harmless slippery fish are present. Make sure swimming is permitted in your chosen body of water, and that it's safe to do so before you jump in. If you're nervous, it can be a good idea to start with a body of water that you're familiar with, and a place where others go regularly. If you do decide to swim in the sea, be sure to check currents and tides are safe, as well as what sea traffic (boats, kayaks or canoes) you might encounter.

2. Unless you're into nude swimming (and why not?), make sure you have good quality swimwear. In the colder months, you might want to consider a wetsuit, depending on where you're thinking of swimming and when. The North Sea is going to be bracing in March and November, to say the least! In summer, the water may still be cold, so it's worth researching the average temperature of the water in your chosen location.

3. Finally, make sure you pack a bag with a large towel so you can dry off afterwards, as well as a bottle of water or a hot drink in a flask. You could also pack a healthy snack, so you can refuel after your adventure.

WELCOME THE SUN

Spring turns to summer with stealth; we often notice that the season has changed somewhere around the middle of May. Waking up early to see sunlight peeping through the bedroom curtains, we look forward to longer days to come, when the temperature will be consistently warmer and the heat will rise over the coming months. As with spring, this seasonal change can make us feel a little out of sorts. We don't feel prepared, our skin is still recovering from the cooler months and dressing in summer clothes can feel downright odd. And though, for a lot of people, summer is their favourite time of year, for others the expectation to be up and energetic at this time of year simply makes them irritated, or even depressed. If you're one of those people, then know that there's no shame in it. Your feelings are valid and the last thing you need is to put pressure on yourself to be happy. But there are a few things you can do to help ease you into summer, and one of them is welcoming the sun.

Watching the sun come up while the rest of the world is asleep is a special bonding ritual. The sun is at its coolest and most gentle, and the light (if you choose the right day) is spectacular. It can have a transformative effect on your state of mind, bringing peace to ward off anxiety and sadness. The intimacy you experience with nature is profound, and your attitude towards the onset of summer will become more accepting and excited.

TIPS FOR SUNRISE THERAPY

1. Choose a morning where the sky is fairly clear: not too cloudy and not raining. That way, you'll get the full benefit of the morning light.

2. In order to catch the dawn, you'll need to get up early. Make sure you go to bed early, and set your alarm for the next morning.

3. If you're an urban dweller, seek out a place in your city or town that is quiet, preferably green and, if possible, high up. If you live in a more rural area, find your favourite place to perch.

4. You could take a packed breakfast, a flask of coffee or tea or another drink. Wear layers you can remove so you're prepared for any change in temperature, and put a rug or blanket in your bag so you can sit comfortably.

5. Don't look directly at the sun, ever. Stand in the path of a sunbeam, close your eyes for a moment and stretch out your arms as though you're embracing the sun.

6. When you get home, make a note of how the experience made you feel – in particular, note how the light affected you. Continue to log your moods as you repeat your sunrise practice. Notice what feelings come up, and what effect your experience has on your general mood.

BEACHCOMBING

Beachcombing on a summer's day is a great way to enjoy the benefits of being by water – the breeze, the tang of salt in the air, the sounds of waves lapping in or out – and to encourage our observational brain and our curiosity. Apart from anything else, it's time out from busy cities, roads, crowds and pollution. But it also offers us something else: the pleasure of examining what's been washed up by the tide, feeling the texture and shape of shells, rocks, fossils and occasionally a message in a bottle cannot be underestimated.

Beachcombing is not the same as 'mud-larking', an organized pursuit for which you usually need a license, and which focuses on the foreshores of city rivers, such as the Thames in London. Beachcombing revolves around natural finds, as opposed to financially valuable finds. You can't take sand from a beach, and in certain parts of the UK, pebble-collecting is illegal, so check whether you're allowed to do this on your chosen beach. For the most part, collecting pebbles and shells – as long as they contain no living organisms – and bits of sea glass (bits of old bottles that have been rounded and smoothed by the sea) are usually fine to look for and take home.

If you're interested in the more serious mudlarking, then check out the official websites to find out how you can get involved and what you need. Proper mudlarks, on the Thames foreshore, for example, require special equipment and permits. But if a simple beachcomb is all you're after, or even simply an observational walk, then a little research into your nearest beaches will suffice. You just need to be aware of any rules or regulations about beachcombing.

Remember, this is not a chore. It's an activity that connects you with the elements, with the sometimes centuries-old rocks and stones on the beach, which will ease all manner of stressful feelings and emotions. It's enough just to walk along the beach on a sunny day.

If you want to make more of a commitment to beachcombing and you live a long way from a beach, you could organise a beachcomb with friends; maybe combine it with a weekend break, or a day trip to the seaside. You'll also need to do a little research into which beaches are ideal for beachcombing – where you can find sea glass, for example – and how you might be able to get creative afterwards with your finds.

SUMMER JOURNAL

Some days, our mood is low and we neither want to be inside or go outside and enjoy the sun. We just don't know what to do with ourselves. The pressure to be enjoying the season builds, and summer feels counter-intuitive: beckoning us out, but making us feel stressed, too. Now is the time to take it easy on ourselves and compromise by sitting outside and writing about our feelings, as well as what we see around us.

If you can relate to the feelings described above, then try starting your day with something comforting: listen to your favourite piece of music, read a couple of chapters of a book you're enjoying, dress in clothes that make you feel comfortable. Take your time and remind yourself that whatever you're feeling is OK. By giving yourself permission to feel the way you do, you'll feel less anxious and tense.

Set aside some time to go outside and write down what's in your head. You don't need to go any further than your garden or balcony (if you have one), but you could also head out to a nearby place that makes you feel lighter and more calm. View the notebook as a friend you're taking out with you. If you can, leave your phone at home; it's tempting to lose yourself in your Twitter, Facebook or Instagram feed when you're feeling low and listless, but although social media can help you to feel less alone, it's the kind of distraction that pushes your feelings away when what you really need to do is sit with your feelings.

Just 20 minutes outside, charting your state of mind, will lift a little of your mental burden, making you feel stronger and calmer.

MAKE A BIRD BATH

If you have enough outside space, a bird bath is another wonderful way of helping our feathered friends, particularly in the summer months when water is more scarce. It's also another way to boost our sense of purpose and morale, combining creativity with environmental commitment. A bird bath will encourage birds such as blackbirds and starlings or wood pigeons to your ledge or garden to keep their feathers clean and in good condition, and watching birds enjoy a bath can be a fun and relaxing way to spend some time. You can buy a birdbath, of course, but it couldn't be easier to make one and you might find it more satisfying.

WHAT YOU'LL NEED

1. A wide, shallow, watertight, dish-shaped object, such as an old-fashioned dustbin lid, with sloping sides. It should have a width of around 30 cm and a maximum depth of 10 cm.

2. Some small rocks or stones – or some gravel.

3. Four bricks for the bath to stand on.

4. Water: collect rainwater or use tapwater.

BUILD YOUR BATH

1. Position your bricks on some grass, and place your dish on top. Make sure you place it on grass or ground where birds can easily see it, but close enough to plant borders and foliage so that they feel safe and can hop into the bushes. If you've got pets, make sure it's out of their reach. Cats love to pounce on birds.

2. Put your stones or gravel in the base of the dish, so that the birds have better grip and don't slip underwater.

3. Fill your dish with water, and make sure you keep it regularly topped up.

JOIN A COMMUNITY GARDEN

A community garden is a space of land where the community can volunteer as gardeners, and learn about horticulture and plant and vegetable growth through activity. These gardens have the dual purpose of cultivating nature and bringing people together in a shared experience, working to nurture the land and soothe minds. They can be found mostly in urban areas – in cities and towns where access to green space is more limited – and have been proven to be extremely beneficial to our physical and mental health. Importantly, they can improve quality of life for those with physical and mental-health issues or disabilities.

Along with growing plants and flowers, community gardens often offer access to other team activities – yoga, drawing, even pottery classes – as well as events for kids. If you want to get yourself, a friend or a relative involved then research the community gardens in your neighbourhood to find out what they offer and when, and how to join. Do also find out what is offered for those with either mental or physical disabilities in terms of access and events.

You are most likely to find a community garden in your nearest decent-sized park. Community-garden volunteers will have to sign up and, since people are increasingly signing up to enriching outdoor activities, there could be a waiting list. Be patient and your time will come.

MAKE A FLOWER CHAIN

Remember the hours you spent as a child, cross-legged on the grass, deep in concentration as you made a daisy-chain necklace, bracelet or crown? The sheer pleasure of losing yourself in creativity? This kind of play is not just an important feature of childhood, it is beneficial in adult life, too. Simple, absorbing activity soothes us, drawing us into the moment and focusing our thoughts only on what we are creating. Daisy-chain mindfulness is a brilliant way to bring calm into our days and restore our sense of play.

REFRESHER COURSE, IF YOU NEED ONE

1. Find a patch of grass that's carpeted with small flowers, such as daises (of all types and colours) and buttercups.

2. Once you have a diverse selection, use your thumbnail to put a slit, about half an inch if possible, into the stem of your flower.

3. Thread the stem of another flower into your half-inch slit, then repeat the process for as many flowers as you want to use for your chain.

4. To complete your chain, make an inch split in your final flower, then thread your original daisy through that, removing a few petals if you need to.

TREE SPOTTING AND PLANTING

Many of the trees around us have been there all our lives, and some existed for centuries before we were born. Just thinking about that puts the natural world and its enduring history into perspective, quietly blowing our minds and grounding us at the same time. Properly observing trees – identifying their different characteristics, feeling awe at their size, at the sprawling branches above us and the roots below that seem to resemble giants' feet – is a joy. Trees are majestic, powerful, delicate, elegant and vital, and, in the summer months, they're often vivid with colour.

Not only do trees make oxygen, cleaning the air and the soil and helping to zap air and noise pollution, they also create shade, provide refuge and make our landscapes beautiful. They are often described as the 'lungs of the earth' and we need to take care of them to secure our future environment. Summer is a great time to embark on your tree education, as you can spend more time outside during this season. Learning about trees may well inspire you to grow them, too. The Victorian era saw lots of large canopy trees planted, such as the oak, silver birch and ash, but their lifecycle is coming to an end, so we need to plant more – particularly in urban areas where traffic and industrial fumes pollute the air.

Luckily there are lots of dedicated organisations and charities that provide guides on tree-identification, telling you what characteristics to look out for and at what time of year. So, if you want to recognise a hazel or hawthorn tree, an elder or English elm, check out websites such as the UK's Woodland Trust.

PLANTING THE FUTURE

To paraphrase a famous saying, to plant a tree is to believe in tomorrow – and it is a wonderful feeling to watch a tree grow. Many people plant trees in their gardens or allotment spaces, but you can grow trees in community gardens and orchards, too, so don't despair if you haven't got an outside space of your own.

Different trees have different needs, such as soil preference, so choose your species carefully depending on what land you plan to grow them on. You can find all the information you need about this from trusted online sites, but take a look around the local area, too; see what's thriving where, and it'll give you a good idea of what will work in your space.

If you're planting in woodland areas, learn about the different roles trees have in supporting the nature and wildlife around them. For example, trees that bear berries, such as rowan, hazel and beech, attract wildlife all year round. Check out which species prevent soil erosion, which are best for livestock to shelter beneath and which help to reduce flooding.

Make sure you get expert advice on how to plant your trees: what you'll need to start, how to nurture your tree and how long it will take to reach maturity. It's lovely to feel that the tree you're planting now will reach full size several generations down the line, but there are plenty of trees that grow more quickly, too, if you're keen to see your tree reach full size.

LET'S GO CAMPING

Studies have shown that an introduction to camping and exposure to nature and the elements in childhood helps equip us for the psychological stresses of adult life. Most of us did it, some of us enjoyed it, many of us moaned about it, but pretty much all of us slept outside at some point during our youth and arrived home invigorated by a few days without TV and polluted city air.

Think of camping as a way to reset your mind and body as you escape the pressure of everyday life and explore your resourcefulness. Studies have shown that camping, as with all prolonged periods of time spent outdoors, improves our cognitive function, lowers stress levels, provides us with the opportunity to be autonomous and bonds us not only with nature, but with the people we take camping with us. When we camp, we develop skills that our ancestors utilised every day, such as making a campfire and giving thought and creativity to what we eat and how we prepare it. There is something primal and profound about working together to feed ourselves and keep ourselves warm in an environment where home comforts are not available.

In the modern world, our thoughts are increasingly focused on our self-image and how we present to others. We are exposed to a huge amount of pressure to look good and behave in a way that conforms to societal norms. Camping pushes away those concerns, diminishing them for a few days, and we emerge from the experience fresher, more confident and more content. If you're new to camping, here are some useful tips to make your trip the best it can be.

CAMPING FOR BEGINNERS

1. Get hold of a tent. There are different types of tents of varying sizes and materials, and if you're planning to travel off-grid, where the terrain is uneven and the weather is volatile, a flimsy tent won't do. It's worth consulting experts, and ideally check out a few tents in person before you buy one. You can find lots of great advice online.

2. There are campsites all over the place, so do some research to find the one that suits you – where the facilities and distance to nearby attractions are just right. If you're planning on spending a few days somewhere more remote, or if you're camping out of season, note how long it will take to reach your location, and make sure you arrive there in daylight.

3. Once you have a tent, do a practice run before you go to ensure the tent is in working order, isn't missing any equipment and that the size is right. Research what essentials you'll need to take with you: you'll need cooking equipment, fuel, food and water supplies, etc. You'll find lots of checklists online.

4. It's best to pitch your tent on flat ground, but this isn't always possible. If you have to pitch on a slope, make sure you sleep with your head uphill. Consider whether you want more shade or sun, and what view you want when you unzip your tent. Would you prefer to see the sunrise in the morning or sunset at night? If it's windy, choose a spot next to a hedgerow to provide some protection.

5. You'll find lots of expert advice online about camping stoves and what you'll need for the length of time you're going, as well as tips on making a safe campfire. As a precaution, take some pre-prepared food with you, in case you arrive at your destination tired, or it's raining heavily.

6. It's a good idea to make a rough activity plan for each day of your trip, such as mountain-climbing, wildflower foraging, forest bathing and sea swimming.

FRUIT PICKING

Though you can technically pick fruit all year round, summer is the ideal time to do it. Spending a day at a fruit farm is a glorious way to engage your senses of sight, smell, touch and sound. There's also the unique satisfaction that comes with picking and foraging for fruit, then turning it into seasonal jams, pickles and chutneys afterwards. You'll need to check what fruits are in season and where you'll need to travel to find them. You'll be able to find information about what's in your area online. Now all you need to know is what to wear and what to pack in your travel bag.

PICKING PREP

1. Make sure you wear clothes you don't mind getting stained, and wear long socks, even in summer, to avoid insect bites.

2. Bring lots of water in ceramic or steel bottles to keep you hydrated.

3. Take sunscreen, insect repellant and workwear gloves to protect you from thorns.

4. Pack baby wipes for sticky hands, but make sure you dispose of them properly, in a bin.

5. Bring your own containers so you can carry your fruit home safely.

6. Check what method of payment the fruit farm accepts before you go. Some farms only accept cash.

While you're picking, tread only in the rows of fruit intended for picking: don't stray into any other areas where other plants may be growing. Try to focus on the moment – on the sounds, sights and smells around you. Put your phone on silent and stash it away in your bag so you aren't tempted to check it; that way, you can focus your full attention on the buzzing of bees and chirping of birds. Once you start to listen to nature's sounds, you'll notice how rich they are.

A CRASH COURSE IN FRUIT

To make sure you're bringing home fruit that will actually be fit for use, here's a quick crash-course in all things fruit.

1. You can pick strawberries before they're completely red, but they need to be very nearly there.

2. You'll know blackberries are perfect for picking if they drop easily when you touch them.

3. The same is true of raspberries – they should quickly detach from their stems when you touch them.

4. Pears should be picked before they're ripe (so when they're yellow) and then kept indoors until they ripen fully.

5. Cherries need to be vivid in colour, heavy and glossy and sweet!

You can, of course, eat your fruit raw, but you might want to make use of it in cooking. Make sure you wash all your fruit as soon as you get in. If you've picked more than one kind of fruit, separate them into different containers. Now you can freeze the fruit and use it later.

You'll find lots of recipes and step-by-step guides for making jam, syrups, chutneys and pie-fillings online.

ANYONE FOR CROQUET?

Croquet may seem like an old-fashioned game, but it's perfect for those who like their exercise low impact and mentally stimulating. Unlike other low-impact games such as golf, croquet does not require buying or renting golf clubs and then hulking them over a course, or investing in club membership. Amateur croquet can be played on any decent-sized patch of grass or lawn, and at any age.

There are several reasons why croquet is good for both physical and mental health. It means spending time outside, the benefits of which are hopefully scored into your brain by now! It's exercise that you won't dread, since it's not too strenuous and focuses on gently stretching your muscles. It's a cerebral game; a little like chess, it involves engaging and improving your strategic brain, and boosts your confidence and self-esteem. And it's a social game, which helps to bond people together.

To find out what equipment you'll need and to see a full list of the rules, visit a specialist online site and get expert advice. Croquet can be played with as few as two people, up to a maximum of six. Each side (or team) has two balls: blue and black against red and yellow. Simply put, the object of the game is to hit your balls through a course of six hoops, in the right sequence and in each direction, and culminates in hitting a centre peg. Whoever completes the course first with both balls wins the game.

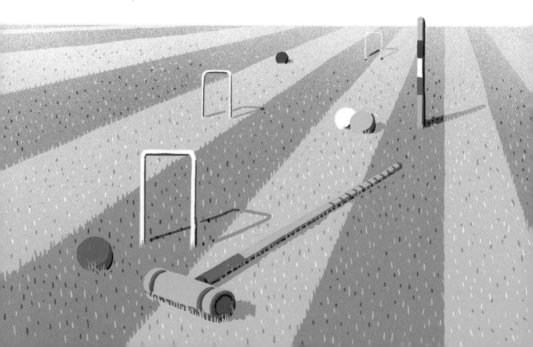

MOONBATHING

Moonbathing has long been used as a
kind of physical therapy, bringing relief to
conditions such as rashes, hives, hypertension
and inflammation, but its effects on our mental
health can't be underestimated, either. The moon's calm,
cooling light slows us down and soothes us, as well as preparing us
for growth. Moonbathing can be done anywhere, even through an open window as
you sit inside your home. Summer is the perfect time for moonbathing, and ideally it
should be done during the waxing (growing) phase of the moon that occurs between
a new moon and a full moon. You can be seated or lying down, with or without
clothes, as you receive the moon's light and healing power. This helps connect us to a
more spiritual side of ourselves, soothing our nervous systems and encouraging us to
stay in the present moment as well as bringing out our important primal emotions.

Bear in mind which phase the moon is in, since its varying light influences our
emotions and state of mind in different ways. When there is a new moon, our minds
absorb more thought and we store more energy. A full moon, on the other hand,
harnesses our more active, creative brain. As in werewolf mythology, we feel more
emotional and feral. A new moon is a time to embrace new beginnings, reflect on
what we want to achieve and set realistic goals. A full moon gives us an opportunity
to reflect on what we have to be thankful for – if we learn to think of ourselves as
lucky, our self-esteem and our sense of contentment increase. Your moonbathing
experience should echo that of meditation and certain yoga practices. Keep your
eyes open as you declutter your mind, focus on your breath and observe the
sensations you experience as you respond to the moon's light.

IMMERSE YOURSELF IN LAVENDER

Lavender doesn't just look pretty and smell heavenly, it is something of a super herb, too! It can be grown everywhere, though it originates in Africa and the Mediterranean, and the oil that is produced from it has a variety of excellent benefits, both cosmetic and healing, for body and mind. It has long been believed to have anti-inflammatory and antiseptic properties, as well as alleviating headaches and digestive issues, and studies suggest that it is an effective treatment for anxiety and insomnia, too. There are lots of reasons to experience the power of lavender. One excellent way of doing that is by visiting a lavender farm or field. These tend to be found in more rural areas, and July is the best time to visit for full bloom lavender. Do check the rules and regulations for your chosen farm or field before you go; each site will have different rules about things like picnics and dogs.

A QUICK GUIDE TO GROWING LAVENDER

1. Lavender blooms in late spring and summer, so April or May is the best time to plant it.

2. Lavender comes in a range of sizes, colours and hardiness-levels, so bear this in mind. English lavender is tougher and better able to endure volatile weather conditions, which means it can be potted and grown in borders. It is strongly aromatic and either purple or purple-blue in summer, with silver-grey leaves.

3. Plant your lavender in sun-absorbing borders or beds, in free-draining soil. Though English lavender is sturdy, it doesn't really like shady or damp conditions. It likes alkaline or chalky soil, not heavy soil such as clay as it retains too much water in winter.

4. If you are growing lavender in a garden, position the plants roughly 90 cm apart. If you want to grow a tightly-packed lavender hedge, space the plants about 30 cm apart.

5. If you're growing lavender in a pot, make sure it has large drainage holes, use loam-based compost and add grit or stones to the bottom.

6. Water regularly – at least once or twice a week, though more often in high summer.

MAKE A SUMMER
FLOWER PRESS

In summer, we're exposed to an abundance of gorgeous flowers. Although there is nothing to beat a fresh flower for its delicacy, life and vivid colour, pressing flowers is a lovely way of extending their life, ensuring they continue to lighten your mood and brighten your home.

You can buy a flower press, but they can be expensive. You can simply buy some parchment paper and create your own, effective press, as follows.

YOUR DIY FLOWER PRESS

1. You'll need a large, heavy book that you don't mind getting damaged, and absorbent paper such as parchment (an art shop or stationers will stock this). You can also use coffee filters or thin cardboard.

2. Remove excess leaves, then place your flowers flat on your paper.

3. With the flowers face-down on your paper, place another piece of paper on top, then place everything between the pages of your book and close the book.

4. Store your book somewhere where it won't be disturbed, and place either another heavy book or a couple of bricks on top of it to add weight to your press.

5. Leave for three to four weeks before removing your flowers and displaying them in your home.

MAKE A MIDSUMMER CROWN

In Sweden, where the winter and spring months are darker and the days shorter, the summer solstice is welcomed in at *Midsommar*. *Midsommar* began as a Pagan ritual, but has evolved into a celebration of longer, brighter days, new life and the emergence from the lowered morale and depression often associated with winter. These days, it isn't just the Swedes who celebrate *Midsommar*. Many other countries have adopted the tradition, and in particular the creation of midsummer floral crowns made of vividly-coloured summer flowers and leaves. Making a headpiece of fresh, aromatic flowers is enjoyable, creative, aesthetically stunning and an instant mood-lifter. You'll just need nature, some secateurs and some thin florist's wire.

HOW TO MAKE YOUR CROWN

1. Search your local wood or park for a fallen branch. The principles for the crown itself are the same as for the spring wreath, though you just need one thin, flexible branch.

2. Select your flowers. Delicate but brightly coloured varieties such as cornflowers, roses and gerbera are great, but there are lots of others to choose from, depending on your taste and whether you have a colour scheme in mind. Make sure to gather some luscious greenery, too, to nestle your flowers in.

3. Shape your branch into a circle that will fit your head, then secure each end with your wire. Be sure to tuck any sharp ends out of the way.

4. Carefully form your flowers and greenery into small bouquets and attach to your crown with wire. You can attach as many of these bouquets as you want – just make sure the flower heads are pointing in roughly the right direction (outwards).

FORAGE FOR ELDERFLOWER

You might have spotted elderflower trees, with their exquisite, lacy, white blossom, decorating hedgerows in the late spring and early summer. And you'll no doubt have smelled their sweet, almost ice-cream-like aroma. For centuries, the elderflower has been believed to have medicinal and healing powers. It is anti-septic, anti-inflammatory and, when combined with water, a traditionally effective antidote to common colds and some types of arthritis. When used in recipes, it has been reported that elderflower has the power to boost mental health and promote a good mood. Armed with secateurs or scissors, set out to find small elderflower trees between June and August; you'll recognise them by their unique flowers and cork-like branches.

HOW TO GATHER AND PREPARE YOUR ELDERFLOWER

1. Before you set off on a forage, first make sure you have permission to wander around your chosen location.

2. It's also a good idea to know what you want to do with your elderflowers – i.e. which recipes you want to try. You can find lots of ideas online, including the well-known cordial and champagne, but why not try the lesser-known elderflower custard or ice-cream? Also, elderflowers and gooseberries are a dream combination, so look up recipes for gooseberry and elderflower crumbles and jams.

3. The leaves and foliage of the elderflower are thought to be mildly poisonous, so be sure you don't bring any home with you.

4. It's best to gather your elderflowers after two or three days of consistent sun. Give them a hearty sniff to make sure they are strongly fragrant, then carefully snip off the flower heads – between 12 and 18 is ideal – and then take them home to use before their aroma starts to fade.

5. Don't wash your elderflowers or you'll strip them of their smell and their flavour. Do pick off any lingering insects, though.

6. Get cooking!

POND DIPPING

Pond dipping is a great way to monitor a pond's biodiversity, take in the beauty of its inhabitants and connect with the natural world. If you're lucky you might spot the predatory, diamond-shaped water scorpion that loiters on banks, the stickleback with its bony armour, the dragonfly or the damselfly, the great diving beetle, a leech or a water snail. Each of these wonderful creatures has its own agenda, and learning to identify them expands your focus, grounds you and cultivates curiosity and respect for nature. Before you embark on a pond dipping expedition, do some online research into nearby ponds and rivers and what you might find there.

You don't need expensive, specialist equipment to pond dip. Here's a checklist of what to know and what to take – you may already have a lot of this at home.

1. If you're a non-swimmer, make sure you take a lifejacket if you're visiting water deeper than five feet. If you have any allergies, check with your doctor before embarking on a pond dip.

2. Make sure you have waterproof boots or shoes, as well as spare socks and a towel to dry your hands.

3. Get hold of a long net – the kind you might have used for crab fishing as a child. These can be bought cheaply online or from a fishing shop if you haven't already got one.

4. You'll also need a sieve – the kind you use for flour. This will help you to explore the mud on the floor of your pond or river.

5. For a DIY aquarium, a good-sized food container will do.

6. Don't forget a magnifying glass, so you can scrutinise your water life.

7. You'll also need a notebook and a pen or pencil to record each of your finds.

8. If you want to take pictures, pack a camera or your phone.

HOW TO POND DIP SAFELY AND RESPONSIBLY

Always approach any pond plants or wildlife with respect, common sense and knowledge of what is and is not acceptable. Here are some guidelines.

1. Make sure you have the permission of whoever owns the pond or lake you want to dip in.

2. Before you set out, wash and thoroughly rinse your hands so that you don't transfer harmful substances to the water.

3. It is illegal to move many species of wildlife from their chosen habitat, so if you're temporarily collecting wildlife for observation, make sure you put it back in the same pond you got it from. This also prevents transfer of bacteria.

4. There will be all kinds of bacteria in the water, so always wear waterproof gloves and cover any cuts or grazes with waterproof plasters to prevent infection.

5. Don't touch your face until you have arrived home and thoroughly washed your hands.

6. Use instruments such as plastic spoons or soft paintbrushes to move pond plants and wildlife. Never use sharp instruments or pipettes that will act as a vacuum.

7. Do some research ahead of your trip, so you can identify carnivore and herbivore wildlife and keep them in separate containers. If you put them in the same container, one might eat the other! As a general rule, don't leave any of your wildlife in your containers too long.

8. When you've finished observing, photographing and making notes about the wildlife you have in your containers, make sure you put them all back where you found them by holding your vessel just beneath the water's surface until they have all escaped.

9. Wash your hands, net, containers, gloves and any of your safe instruments thoroughly when you get home to avoid spreading bacteria.

BUTTERFLY SPOTTING

Out of all of nature's extraordinary wildlife, the butterfly is the most artfully and exquisitely patterned, so elegant and agile. Butterflies are emblematic of the summer months, a testament to nature's beauty and a symbol of transformation. Perhaps that's why glimpsing one fluttering past can make us feel lighter, happier and more hopeful. And butterfly spotting is good for our nervous system; it's a natural pacemaker, slowing us down and encouraging us to wonder at, and be humbled by, the natural world. Anyone can learn how to spot the many different varieties, and there are over sixty in the UK alone. No special equipment is required, but it's worth consulting expert resources to help you create a butterfly checklist. Then, all you need is time, a watchful eye and a little bit of patience.

HOW TO SPOT BUTTERFLIES

1. Find a garden, park, field or nature reserve to do your butterfly study.

2. The naked eye is perfectly good for this activity, but if you do decide you want to use binoculars, an inexpensive pair will more than suffice.

3. It can take years to spot and identify all the different types of butterfly, since they can be quite elusive. Don't feel frustrated if you only see a few varieties, or even just one, on your first few tries. There's no rush, just keep your checklist of colours, sizes, shapes and markings with you.

4. Butterflies are frightened off by shadows, so you're most likely to see them in the middle of the day when shadows are smallest. Try to position yourself in a place where you don't cast a shadow, and don't make any sudden movements or they will quickly flutter off.

5. If you're butterfly spotting in your garden, bear in mind that the type of plants you have will determine whether butterflies will visit. Plants such as buddleia, marjoram and Michaelmas daisies are butterfly magnets.

CLOUD HUNTING

Yes, it is a thing! There is a lot to know about those strange, beautiful, puffy shapes above us, and cloud hunting couldn't be easier. Just find a spot with an unobstructed view of the sky and settle in to watch the show.

Low clouds are formed from tiny droplets of water, and those higher up are made of ice crystals. There are 10 types of cloud, categorised by their appearance, what form they take (some are made of layers, some of individual clumps) and where in the sky they sit: low, middle or high. If you visit meteorological sites online, find one that has a comprehensive cloud-spotting guide with information on what to look for. Learning to distinguish a Cumulus from a Cumulonimbus will add to your awe of the amazing world you're living in.

Once you've learned how to identify the different types of clouds, you'll see the sky in a different way. This knowledge will encourage a new appreciation for this aspect of nature. And for weather watchers, identifying certain clouds in the sky – such as Cirrus clouds and Altostratus clouds – gives you a good idea of when to expect rain or warmer weather. Research the various clouds and what their appearance means, and create a visual checklist to keep on your phone.

BEFRIENDING OUR BEES

At one point or another, many of us have viewed bees as pesky insects with a deadly sting that we want to get away from. But that's all changing now that we know bees are endangered. Bees play a vital part in nature, and in all our lives; they are super pollinators of fruit, nuts and vegetables, and without them our food supply is threatened. We need bees, and they need us. In nurturing them we are also improving our mental health; studies show that beekeeping significantly alleviates conditions like anxiety, depression and even PTSD. It reduces stress and harnesses our community and environmental spirit.

Beekeeping is a hugely rewarding activity, and it's accessible for all ages and budgets. If you're nervous about getting involved, you can start by paying a visit to a nearby beekeeping farm or facility. These can be found in urban areas such as in parks, as well as in more rural areas. Observe the tranquility of bee care, and marvel at the characteristics and social hierarchy of these important insects.

Bees are ruled by females. A bee colony is formed of one queen bee, a few hundred male bees (also known as drones) and tens of thousands of worker bees (up to about fifty thousand). The worker bee (or honeybee) is the kind you often see outdoors. The queen bee is big – larger than a worker bee – and has a lifespan of about three years. In her lifetime, she will lay over half a million eggs and mate with around half a dozen drones, who die once they've fulfilled their duty. The queen then buzzes off to the hive where she is served by worker bees.

Educating ourselves about bees is a great start to our beekeeping lives. There's plenty more to learn from the experts, both online and at farms, but here's a practical checklist to get you started.

WHAT TO KNOW ABOUT BEEKEEPING AND HONEY FARMING

1. If you're willing and able to create your own beekeeping facility, you'll need to buy a hive. The best and simplest one for beginners is known as a National, and resembles a brown cardboard box. If you're after one that looks more like a traditional hive, then the WBC hive is often a double layered white hive, which is a little more complicated to work with.

2. You'll need protective clothing, gloves, a veil and footwear. Check online for an outfit that encompasses all these essentials – there are plenty of affordable options.

3. You'll need bees, of course! Check out your local beekeepers' association, who will sell them, or you can buy bees at auction – just search for classified adverts for the next open auction. If you're a beginner, it's important to remember that bees, like humans, come with different temperaments. Ask the breeder to find you a gentle colony, rather than a more aggressive colony.

4. You'll need to invest in a smoker for the hive, which mimics a forest fire and signals to the bees that they should start eating honey, leaving you free to tend to the hive. You'll also need a hive tool to prise apart the hive compartments.

5. Though you can leave your bees to get on with it most of the time, in warmer weather you should clean your hive thoroughly, check that your queen is laying eggs and make sure you have enough honey stores. Your colony will grow fast up until about July and the hive can become overcrowded if you don't keep an eye on it. If that happens, the queen may take a group of her drones and start a new colony somewhere else.

6. August is the time to collect your honey, when most flowers have bloomed. You can harvest up to 40 pounds of it! In the autumn, make sure you compensate your bees for this loss by feeding them a sugar-solution substitute.

INSECT WATCH

Insects, also known as arthropods, get a bad rap. As adults, we're accustomed to viewing them as a nuisance, not as the environmentally-useful creatures they really are. Our squeamishness around insects is a learned response that evolves as we grow from infancy to adulthood. Our child selves had no negative preconceptions of insects; in fact, we invariably found them riveting, and would happily watch them for hours. Now is the time to channel that curiosity again, because observing insects opens our eyes to the world of colour, amazing shapes, interesting behaviour and diversity of our arthropod friends. When we take time to study them, we see them transform and adapt and understand how they function as part of the ecosystem. Importantly, we'll connect to nature and develop our environmental awareness as well as learning a few things about insects' powers of communication, organisation and adaptability. And a little research will really open your eyes to the way in which things like pesticide use and climate change affect these vital players in the natural world.

Make the leap and discover a huge variety of insects you never knew existed. To really broaden your knowledge, look out for the unfamiliar, such as the vapourer caterpillar with its orange-and-brown striped mohawk, the gorgeous emerald damselfly found near ponds and lakes, the orange ladybird, the violet ground beetle, the green tiger beetle, the flat-backed millipede or the Alder fly. These and lots more vivid insects can be found from summer through to autumn.

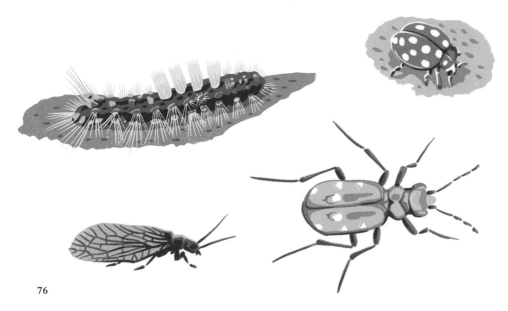

TIPS FOR INSECT OBSERVATION

1. There are a few verified nature observation websites, which will tell you all you need to know about insects: their characteristics, colouring and when and where to spot them. Arm yourself with this information before you begin your insect watch.

2. If you'd like to capture some insects for more thorough observation, you'll need some containers. Clear plastic containers, or glass jars with paper lids held by elastic bands will do, as long as they're big enough for the insect to move around in. Make sure you punch holes in the containers so that the insect(s) can breathe, and keep the containers moist, either by spraying a mist of water inside, or putting a damp sponge in the bottom.

3. If you can get your hands on a magnifying glass, this will allow you to study the insects in even greater detail.

4. Keep your insect captive for a short time only – 10 minutes to half an hour – then release it back where you found it.

BAT WALKING

You might think bats are the stuff of horror films, circling haunted houses at a full moon, but bats are a force for good. If you're one of those people who is a magnet for midges in the summer, just remember it could be a lot worse without bats, whose mission is to catch and eat up to 70,000 midges (per bat). They are also physically fascinating, and often quite cute. Bat walks are increasingly popular in the summer months, and have been known to inspire romance. Suggesting a bat walk for a first date is a great way of nurturing companionable silence and calm and creating a magical experience as you get in touch with nature.

You can research the kind of bats you might spot beforehand, and you can take this information with you when you set off, but in built-up areas you will find the *Pipistrelle* species, which fly out just before and around sunset. Make sure you know when the sun is going to set on your chosen day.

WHAT TO KNOW BEFORE YOUR BAT WALK

1. You'll need to dress in comfortable, waterproof clothes, and make sure you have a torch.

2. It's quite easy to find an organised bat tour near to you, but you can also devise your own. If you live in an urban area, research places of vegetation (tree-lined or park areas) that cut through or run alongside rivers or canals. Though bats also gather in buildings, they are hard to access. If you're a countryside dweller, take a walk along a woodland edge or path where there are more open areas of land. As a rule, wherever there are a lot of insects flying about, there will be bats, too.

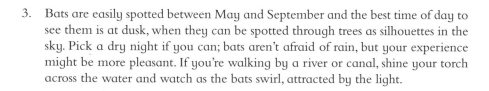

3. Bats are easily spotted between May and September and the best time of day to see them is at dusk, when they can be spotted through trees as silhouettes in the sky. Pick a dry night if you can; bats aren't afraid of rain, but your experience might be more pleasant. If you're walking by a river or canal, shine your torch across the water and watch as the bats swirl, attracted by the light.

CARING FOR FROGS

Frogs and toads can be found anywhere where there are ponds and lakes as they thrive in or around water. Making sure their environment is maintained is a wonderful way of helping our ecosystem, as well as our own mental health, thanks to the valuable sense of purpose that comes with nurturing nature.

Frogs are vital for our ecosytem as well as our health. They help control the insect population, and they are an important food source for larger wildlife. They also secrete substances through their skin, some of which have been used by scientists to produce human antibiotics and painkillers. Others are poisonous, which is why you should never touch a frog without protection, and keep your pets away from them, too.

In an effort to dodge being eaten, frogs are often on the run, are experts at playing dead and have developed clever camouflage techniques. The *Physalaemus nattereri*, or 'four-eyed frog', has two eyes on its head and two fake eyes (spots) near its back legs, which make it look like a more predatory animal. Frogs are increasingly threatened by environmental change: water pollution, changing temperatures and acid rain. Many urban parks and wetland centres provide safe spaces for frogs, and signpost where to spot them. So, if you haven't got a garden and are wary of trampling on or coming across frogs without warning, these are great places to see them in a more controlled environment. But you can create a home for frogs in your garden pond, if you have one. Here's what to do.

1. Make sure your pond is in a shaded area, but without too many overhanging trees, as it will need some sun to survive.

2. A pond depth of 2 to 3 feet is ideal, with shallow edges so that frogs can get in and out easily.

3. Populate the water with plants such as duckweed, water lilies and marsh marigolds, as well as bordering your pond with plants to create the perfect breeding environment for frogs.

4. Once your frogs have started to spawn and breed, don't move them into a new pond and risk spreading bacteria.

5. Make sure you research what protective clothing or equipment you might need for frog breeding before you start.

WATCH THE SUN SET

Of all the natural sights, a sunset is perhaps the most spectacular, particularly when viewed on the sea's horizon or as it slowly sinks behind a mountain. A sunset has the power to transform our mood, pushing daily stress and anxiety further away and inspiring us as we take in the power of something so much bigger than ourselves making its presence felt from so far away.

The red and orange colours are a result of the daytime's blue light dispersing, leaving only the red light – keeping this in mind adds to the awe. In summer, the days are longer and the sky tends to be clearer, and this is the perfect time to make watching the sun set part of your daily routine. Follow these tips to make it a magical experience.

1. The sun sets in the west, so now's the time to hone your sense of direction. If you are unable to go out, and you live in a property with a high-up window-view of the west, then you can watch the sun set from indoors.

2. Find out what time the sun is going to set, and make sure you position yourself accordingly. Remember, never look directly at the sun.

3. If you choose to watch the sun set outside, over or near to water, the light will be reflected and it intensifies the visual experience. If you live near a lake, river or the sea, head there for a truly magical sunset experience.

4. Use your magical sunset experience to inspire gratitude for the beauty of nature. This provides important perspective on the world around us and our place in it.

AL FRESCO DINING

In summer, eating outside at any time of day is a glorious experience, but creating an al fresco dinner party is a wonderful end to a summer's day. Having your own private garden is a privilege not everyone enjoys, but even without one you can still enjoy eating outside. Here's how.

1. If you live in a city, check closing times for your local parks (they often stay open till it gets dark) and consult a weather app so you can avoid a rainy or overcast evening.

2. If you're the organiser/host, and you can afford it, shop for picnic-style seasonal food. You can spread the food out as a banquet to create a more informal eating experience where everyone can chat as they graze.

3. If you're on a budget, why not try a pot luck dinner, where each guest brings a contribution of food and drink. You can provide seating and a table if you're in your garden, but sitting on a groundsheet allows you to be closer to nature, and further enhances the experience.

4. If the weather is dry and warm, eating outside is lovely at any time of day, so extend your al fresco dining experience to breakfast, lunch or tea. Whether you enjoy these alone or with family and friends is up to you.

5. To ward off insects such as mosquitoes, wear a long-sleeved shirt or T-shirt and cover your legs and ankles. If it's too hot for long sleeves, invest in a recommended insect repellant and, if you are particularly allergic to insect bites, keep allergy medication nearby.

BECOME A NATURE CONSERVATION VOLUNTEER

With your discovery of the extraordinary natural world, and the positive effect it has had on your general wellbeing, you may be ready to take a more active part in its conservation. Whether you have a special interest in animals, plant life or climate change, there are volunteer programmes for you. You may have to wait to secure a place as a volunteer, but it'll give you something to look forward to.

Volunteer programmes are available for both national and overseas work. If you want to combine travel with nature preservation, you could be heading for far-flung countries in Africa or South America. Seeing the world whilst simultaneously working towards global conservation can be a life-transforming experience. But if you're more of a homebody, then there is a huge amount you can do in your own country. Here are some ideas.

1. Sign up for nature-reserve care, plant identification or GPS mapping.

2. Set up a wildlife-watch team, inviting friends or teenagers to participate in nurturing your local environment.

3. Survey species: search for otters or go on a seal watch to learn from experts about the important part these animals have to play in our rivers, seas and oceans. You can make a contribution to their preservation by identifying them in time-lapse and drone photographs.

4. Observe hedgehogs, go on a slug hunt or complete a flatworm or farm wildlife survey. Registering to help with your local park's upkeep or forest restoration is ideal for those who can't travel far but want to get involved and spend more time outside.

5. For anyone who is housebound or physically disabled, there is a valuable contribution to be made by offering your IT or technology, administrative or financial skills to help the cause. This means you can work from home and still reap the positive benefits of helping keep the natural world thriving and healthy.

SUMMER PHOTOSHOOT

As the summer draws to a close it can bring on melancholy or low mood. This may be associated with childhood, when the long summer holidays were a time for fun, play and family time. They generally involved long weeks spent with people we love, where the stresses and strains of school work were replaced by hours outdoors in the sun. For many people, the end of summer means the beginning of more structured, less relaxing daily life. The world may seem a little dimmer and we may feel there is less to look forward to.

One way to help combat the end-of-summer blues is to look back on the season through a visual record. The longer, dryer days of summer provide ample opportunity for visual journalling, and with the sophisticated cameras many of us have in our phones, photographing our summer experience couldn't be easier. As with memories of our spring nature journey, we can create a summer album with a dedicated Instagram or Facebook account, or simply keep our memories to ourselves. It can be useful to note down how we feel with every outdoor experience, in relation to the effect it may have had on our mental or physical wellbeing, and which details stood out as particularly joyful or fascinating. Any activities which move us out of our comfort zone and challenge us mentally and physically will undoubtedly teach us something useful.

GETTING THE MOST OUT OF YOUR PHOTOSHOOT

1. Make sure your camera is charged before you set off for an activity. You can either take a notebook to write down significant thoughts or feelings, or use the notes section of your phone.

2. Thinking about all of your senses, be alert for anything that stops you in your tracks or brings about feelings of calm and happiness – these are the things you'll want to stop and photograph. It could be the sound of birdsong in the morning, the sight of a magnificent tree, a glorious abundance of lavender, even a snail slowly making its way across a path. You may also want to photograph yourself in various locations to help you remember the feelings you felt as you explored.

3. Notice the colours of the sky, the grass, the vivid green of tree leaves and the incredible flowers that bloom in this season.

4. Capture summer sunsets in a few different locations. Note the variance in colours each time.

AUTUMN

AUTUMN HEALING

As summer draws to a close, nature begins the process of regrowth. Seeds and leaves drop from the trees and are absorbed back into the earth, enriching the soil and enabling new life. Summer is autumn's hedonistic cousin, parading its glorious, vibrant colours and blazing from the start of June right through to September. At the end of summer's reign, nature needs to quieten down and rest. The air needs purifying, and its wildlife, flowers, plants and leaves adapt for the long months of winter. Autumn is when nature lays itself bare and, in this way, it echoes our own cyclical process: we can feel a sense of loss and melancholy at this time. Our energy slows, the sun is dimmer and the air pollutants that were prevalent over the summer have taken their toll. Just like a tree stripped of its leaves, we feel more emotionally vulnerable and exposed in the autumn months, and we naturally crave comfort.

It can be tough to feel motivated when all we really want to do is curl up indoors with a good book, but spending time engaging with the nature healing around us will heal us, too. This is the time to gently prepare ourselves for winter and focus on building good physical and mental health.

HOW TO PRACTISE AUTUMN HEALING

1. Work on your breathing. Set an alarm, get up while the day is still quiet and find a familiar outside space (your garden, a yard, a field or a park) to spend time giving your lungs a gentle workout in the crisp, autumn air. Sit or stand in a comfortable position and take moderately deep breaths in and out. Notice the sensation as the air comes in and out of your lungs. Repeat, and this time let your stomach move in with your inhalations and out with your exhalations. During this exercise, try to make these in-out breaths continuous (no breaks) for up to 10 minutes.

2. Choose exercise and activities that will strengthen and expand your lungs, such as swimming or singing. These will help to open your chest and shoulders. You'll feel your body becoming stronger and, just as importantly, you'll feel anxiety, stress or sadness diminish.

3. Eat to nourish your lungs. Highly flavoured natural foods such as cinnamon, ginger, almonds, chillies and garlic are important for clearing and cleaning our lungs and digestive systems, and triggering good kidney and liver function, stimulating healthy blood flow and good heart health.

4. Noticing how we feel every day helps to declutter and unburden our mind. Start with the fact that no feelings are negative – it's vital that we respond emotionally to changing seasons, our relationships and our environment. There is no good or bad way to feel, and in respecting ourselves this way, we are strengthening our resilience and preparing for what each day brings. This is particularly important in seasons when the outside world can seem less welcoming. Autumn is there to embrace and heal us – all we have to do is adapt to and embrace it in return.

EMBRACE THE EQUINOX

The autumn equinox, which occurs in September each year, is one of the two occasions annually when the sun illuminates both the northern and southern hemispheres and affects the moon and the stars, giving off a distinct light. In Pagan tradition, the autumn equinox is a celebration of the harvest, with a focus on sharing the fruits of the Earth and celebrating community. In Japan, the equinox is marked by a ritual called *Higan*, which lasts seven days and is a time to mourn and remember friends and family who've passed away.

The full moon that occurs nearest to the equinox is known as a Harvest Moon, so called because, historically, the light it produced meant farmers could work late in the evening to bring in the harvest. Since dates for the equinox vary from year to year, check the timing, then make a date to watch the Harvest Moon in all its splendour. For  star and sky gazers in the high northern-hemisphere latitudes, the autumn equinox means there's a good chance of seeing the aurora borealis.

However you're feeling, keep in mind that the equinox is an ideal time to focus on decluttering our lives, on slowing down a little and on reflecting. We need this time to prepare for the winter to come, and to take care of ourselves. Making time to take in the glorious golds, reds and browns of autumn, and giving thanks for what you have, brings a sense of calm and pleasure. It reminds us that, within all challenging situations, pockets of joy and positivity can be found.

YOUR AUTUMN EQUINOX MENU

Celebrate the equinox by cooking warming, nourishing meals, making the most of autumn's fruit and vegetables. Here are a few tips to inspire you.

1. Notice the vivid colours outside, and incorporate them into your diet. Try vegetables such as squash, carrots and beetroot, all of which contain important antioxidants, vitamin C and anthocyanidins – mineral compounds that maintain our immune systems and circulation – along with seasonal fruit such as russet apples. Spend time making soothing soups, quiches or winter salads.

2. Give your system a zing with spices such as ginger, turmeric and cayenne pepper. These are great immunity-boosting additions to meals.

3. You'll find blackberries in abundance this time of year. Not only are they seductively dark and pretty, they are an excellent source of vitamin C (important in fighting off bacteria), a gentle anti-inflammatory and some studies show that they help stabilise blood sugar, too. So many delicious dishes can be made from these multi-purpose fruits: ice cream, compotes, crumbles – and adding them to your porridge in the morning will brighten your breakfast and your mood.

TREASURE AUTUMN FALL

Of all the seasons, it is arguably autumn that creates the most striking visual feast. Reds, rusts, golds and browns swirl together to make a spectacular montage of colour. As the months grow cooler and the mornings chillier, the sight of frost is almost magical.

We can combat the end-of-summer blues by enjoying these rich colours, the conkers and acorns that are scattered on the ground, the incredible design of leaves, breathtaking even when it is damp, misty or muddy. The treasures of autumn will bring cosiness and warmth to your home, too, when used as decorations or photographed and framed. Explore your creativity and try these methods of turning autumn treasures into works of art.

1. Collect acorns, dry them and then position and glue them around an existing photo or picture frame. You can use paints or ink to add some colour, too.

2. If you're ready for something a little avant garde, spend some time building a collection of different leaves, then use spray paint to add silver, gold, pink or blue to their tips. Arrange and press inside a perspex picture frame.

3. For an autumn dinner party, fill a shallow bowl with a little water and place leaves on top. Put a tea light in the centre and position on your table to give autumnal warmth to the festivities.

4. For gorgeous window decorations, gently pierce a hole through the stems of your leaves, and thread cotton through, then use reusable adhesive or putty to attach them to the top of your window. On a sunny day, the light shining through the golds and reds will create cosy, autumn light.

5. Add some sparkle to your leaves with spray glitter, and either hang them or scatter them over counters and tabletops to create natural glamour.

6. Conkers are a lovely alternative to pot pourri for bathroom or bedroom decoration. Arrange them in a good-sized shallow metal or ceramic bowl, preferably one that contrasts with their colour and texture.

LEAF LANTERN

You can make gorgeous, safe leaf lanterns using leaves, greaseproof paper, a little glue and a battery-operated tea light. Here's how:

1. Collect your leaves – a mix of different sizes and colours work best – and dry them between old newspaper.

2. For the base of your lamp, use the lid of a tubular container; a coffee-tin lid or a cheese container (the kind camembert comes in) will be the ideal size.

3. Take two sheets of greaseproof paper. Cut and shape them into the right size of tube to fit your base, then place one sheet over the other. This doubles the thickness of your shade and makes it sturdier.

4. Now, lay your 2-ply paper flat and carefully glue your leaves on to the paper in any position you want. The more random the placement, the better.

5. Once the glue has dried, carefully wrap your leaf paper into a tube and glue or staple it together.

6. Glue the bottom of your leaf shade to the base, and leave to dry.

7. Carefully lower your battery-operated tea light down onto the centre of your base. Make sure you can easily remove it when you want to.

VOLUNTEER AT AN URBAN ORCHARD

As with community gardening, learning to plant, grow and harvest fruit trees provides us with invaluable benefits and skills, including an appreciation of nature through active nurturing, physical exercise and team work. Working as part of a gardening co-operative encourages our sense of community, and engages us in a hugely satisfying activity – one that encourages us to look beyond ourselves to the bigger picture of the natural world and its vital importance in our lives and for our wellbeing.

Some orchard projects cultivate fruit, harvest it, then use it to make meals for those in need in the community. Others turn under-used land into green spaces, bringing nature to city areas and pleasure to residents who might have little access to nature otherwise. Whatever the aim, volunteering as an orchard gardener will reap benefits, such as a sense of achievement and improved self-esteem, along with your appreciation of community. If you feel isolated or lonely, becoming part of an orchard team will help you bond and form relationships with all kinds of people from different backgrounds, bringing friendship to a valuable ecological activity.

WHAT'S INVOLVED

1. You'll be helping to nurture community orchards in housing estates, parks, prisons, hospitals, schools and other public spaces.

2. Many organisations provide training and support in developing your gardening, management, fruit processing, harvesting and apple and pear identification skills. This helps you become more self-reliant.

3. It's an education in organic plant disease and pest control.

4. Being part of a public orchard-growing team, you'll be making the space a focal point for community life and a celebration of nature.

5. You'll learn how to turn orchard produce into food for the marketplace.

If volunteering at an orchard feels like too much of an undertaking, you can still enjoy the fruits of its harvest. Though most fruit ripens in the summer months, mid-season apples, elderberries, plums, raspberries and strawberries are still delicious in September and October. In November, there are plenty of mid-season apples that are good to eat. Give the supermarket a miss and experience the pleasure of hand-picking your own fruit at your nearest orchard instead.

HELP OUT AT A CARE FARM

Care farms are wonderful places for people of all ages, abilities and backgrounds to visit or volunteer at. Spending time with animals is known to lower anxiety and increase your sense of independence and achievement. The gentle, companionable nature of animals, who respond to kindness and nurturing rather than physical or mental characteristics, is soothing and joyful.

There are care farms across the country, and many city farms function as care farms, too, so you don't have to travel far to get involved. Here are some of the great benefits if you do decide to give this a try.

1. Helping out at a care farm is sociable and community driven. If you suffer from loneliness, or are shy or introverted, volunteering at a care farm brings you together with like-minded people for a really worthwhile purpose. Learning to care for the animals together provides an instant conversation starter, and, if you're not the chatty kind, then working in companiable silence is also a soothing, stress-relieving activity.

2. You'll get to observe animals such as rabbits, goats, chickens, horses and pigs at close quarters. You'll be learning how to understand their behaviour and their needs, getting to know their characters, learning how to be around them and delighting in their growing trust in you.

3. Spending time outside is always a good thing, particularly in areas of low pollution. Fresh air and exercise, along with the unique sense of achievement you get from caring for other living creatures, will have noticeably positive effects on your mind and your body.

When the time is right, investigate care farms local to you or, if you're willing to travel further afield, those out of your area. There may be a waiting list, but if there is, simply think of it as something to look forward to.

DONKEY THERAPY

These strong, intelligent, good-natured and calm animals are quiet superheroes. Donkeys can live for up to 50 years. They're very strong – stronger than horses of the same size, in fact. And they have incredible memories – they are able to recognise places and other donkeys that they haven't seen for decades. Along with these superskills, studies show that donkeys are hugely therapeutic animals – particularly for the physically and mentally disabled and those who suffer with issues such as depression, anxiety and dementia. For people suffering from Alzheimer's disease, spending time with donkeys can help reduce feelings of isolation and loneliness and the distress associated with this condition. Connecting with donkeys really is a multi-beneficial experience, as well as an adorable and soothing outdoor activity.

There are lots of donkey sanctuaries that you can visit. It is also possible, if you have the budget, to hire a donkey to come and visit you for the day. And though donkey rides on beaches are less available than they were, you may still be able to find donkey-ride fun if you do your research online – for this and for sanctuaries and visiting times near you.

SPOT A STARLING MURMURATION

A starling murmuration is the term given to flocks of starlings who gather and swoop together, silhouetted in the sky, creating spectacular shapes. There are various theories as to why starlings perform this breathtaking ritual, which usually occurs from mid-October to mid-November. There is safety in numbers, and the murmuration is a protective measure against other, predatory birds such as falcons. Massed together, the starlings have a hypnotic effect on enemy birds, making it difficult for them to be targeted individually. Huddling together also keeps them warm, and it's believed that they also communicate important information on where to feed. The murmuration also seems to be a ritual of whirling and swooping that starlings perform before they roost for the night. Even without any clear function, a starling murmuration is a sight to behold, and a lovely show of bird theatre. If you make the effort to catch sight of one this season, here's what you should know.

1. As autumn progresses, more and more starlings gather for a murmuration. So, for the largest and most dramatic performances (sometimes up to 10,000 birds), pencil this activity in for late November.

2. The best time to spot them is just before dusk. You don't need any special equipment; the naked eye will be more than adequate.

3. Starlings tend to roost where there is shelter from colder, harsher weather and predatory birds. At night-time, they may head to woodlands, cliffs or tall, industrial buildings. During the day, treetops are favourite spots; here they can settle and enjoy a panoramic view.

TAKE UP TAI CHI

Aerobic exercise is great for our physical and mental health. The endorphins produced when we push ourselves this way make us feel more positive and energetic, and we sleep better. But there are vital psychological benefits to lower-impact exercise that focuses on core strength, improved posture, flexibility and breathing, too.

Exercising outdoors, surrounded by nature, is a great way to make yourself feel good. Tai Chi is an ancient martial arts and self-defence practice, and is often referred to as meditation in motion. It's an ideal outdoor exercise and perfect for when the weather is a little cooler. If high-impact running or cycling aren't your thing, but you want to get physically fitter and mentally stronger, seek out Tai Chi classes near you. In the meantime, arm yourself with some knowledge of the power of Tai Chi.

HOW TAI CHI BOOSTS MENTAL HEALTH

1. Life can be hectic, and taking time out to slow down and press our body's reset button through the movements of Tai Chi can relieve stress and anxiety.

2. The measured, controlled movements give us vital awareness of how our body feels – calming us and making us feel more stable and in control.

3. Often, our bodies and minds are out of sync, but Tai Chi creates harmony between them, making us calmer, grounded and at one with ourselves.

4. The core strength we develop through Tai Chi is mentally empowering, improving our resilience and resourcefulness.

PRACTISE YOGA OUTSIDE

Yoga is another fantastic exercise to enjoy surrounded by nature outside. Like Tai Chi, yoga is a slower, meditative practice, and its breathing techniques pull you out of your sympathetic nervous system (fight or flight mode) and into your parasympathetic nervous system (rest and digest mode). It also centres you, helping you to process and then let go of difficult emotions like anger and sadness.

You can find several yoga techniques that are perfect to practise outside, but here are a few to get you started.

1. The Triangle Pose: This is one of the most popular full-body yoga poses and involves a full stretch of our legs and arms while gently twisting our torso. It requires space, which means it's ideal for outdoors, where the fresh air will also assist our breathing.

2. Sun Salutation: First developed as a spiritual tribute to the sun's restorative qualities, the sun salutation is unsurprisingly intended to be performed outdoors and is a series of warm-up poses designed to strengthen our limbs and our core (our spine and skeleton).

3. The Low Lunge Pose: This is thought to be one of the most freeing (loosening) poses in the hatha yoga discipline. It's an excellent pose for stretching hip flexors, relieving tension and improving posture, and a great outdoor warm up for a walk, hike or run.

GET A PET

There are myriad reasons why caring for domestic animals is good for our mental wellbeing. Pets have evolved to become attuned to our emotions, our voices and our body language; many can sense when we are sad or worried and offer comfort. Though most people choose dogs and cats as pets, there are many other options. Rabbits, hamsters, guinea pigs and fish all bring out our nurturing side, taking our focus off ourselves in the most delightful way. Here's a breakdown of the benefits of pet ownership.

1. Pet owners are less likely to suffer from depression and tend to have lower blood pressure than those without pets.

2. When you play with your pet, your serotonin and dopamine levels become elevated. These hormones make you feel happier and more relaxed.

3. If you live alone, cuddling a pet will fulfill your basic human need for sensory touch and affection.

4. You'll spend much more time outside if you have a dog, which will lead to increased vitamin D levels and more time spent in green spaces. And you'll become part of the dog-owner community and discover a whole new friendship group.

RESCUE OR FOSTER AN ANIMAL

There are a few good reasons to adopt a pet. When you adopt a pet from a registered rescue centre, you are giving a neglected, perhaps traumatised, animal a loving home and giving yourself a sense of purpose and increased self-esteem. Rescue pets are every bit as valuable and adorable as those from breeders. By nurturing them and offering them stability, you will gain an important sense of responsibility and a whole lot of love, as well as fresh air and exercise. There are, however, important things to bear in mind before you make the leap.

1. Fostering or adopting an animal is a serious undertaking. Although they are a wonderful antidote to loneliness, as the saying goes: 'they're not just for Christmas'. While cats, hamsters, goldfish and rabbits are relatively low-maintenance, dogs (and particularly puppies) often need more patience and love. Remember that someone likely abandoned them once before, and they may act up as part of their trauma. Be sure you are ready to take that on for more than just a couple of months.

2. Think about your circumstances. The size of your home and whether or not you have a garden are important considerations when it comes to getting pets. Most dogs and cats like a garden to play in, so if you live in a small flat with no outdoor space, adopting a lively pet is not going to work. And though animals often like being around children, those who haven't received much love may be more needy, and compete with children for attention. There are rescue animals for all kinds of living situations, but check carefully to make sure you are getting the right pet for your lifestyle.

3. There will be a small fee for most rescue pets, and you need to factor in vet fees and insurance, as well as food for your animal.

If taking on a dog or cat permanently is too much of an undertaking, consider fostering one for a limited period. There are many domestic animals whose owners aren't able to take care of them at specific times, or who are waiting for a permanent owner to take them. You can also borrow an animal for a day or two. People heading off on holiday or business trips often prefer lending their pet to a home-owner rather than putting them in kennels or cat sanctuaries. Check out information on both of these options online – just make sure the website is officially accredited.

ALL THE PRETTY HORSES

We've grown up reading adventure stories in which horses and ponies were central characters. Many of us either learned or longed to ride these incredible animals, so that we could experience the romance and heroism associated with them.

Engaging with animals encourages our caring brain, taking our focus off ourselves and, in the case of domestic pets such as cats and dogs, experiencing the daily companionship and comfort they offer. But horses play an especially important role in improving our mental wellbeing. Since the 1950s, equine therapy has been used as a treatment for a variety of psychological conditions, such as addiction, autism, anxiety, PTSD, low self-esteem and low confidence.

Since equine therapy is not cheap, it is not possible for everyone to experience it. But we can still discover the significant mental health benefits horses provide and experience first-hand their special powers. Here are a few ideas.

1. If it's riding lessons you're after, you can investigate some beginners' classes by doing a little research into facilities near you. Stables can be found in cities and towns, as well as in the countryside. Horse riding is an exhilarating exercise for your mind and body – it's a great way to get to know these wonderful, majestic creatures, adapt to their natures and gain confidence around them.

2. You can volunteer at a stable that helps the disabled interact with horses. These courses are usually charity-run and reliant on community help with mucking out, grooming and exercising their horses.

3 You can help out at a horse sanctuary where the focus is on rehabilitating and providing a home for horses, some of whom may have been rescued from harmful environments. Contacting your nearest sanctuary to become a volunteer is a great way of putting a positive flag down for the future. And if you are able to, make a donation towards much-needed horse equipment, supplies and the costs of the sanctuary's full time staff.

BUILD A WILDLIFE HOTEL

With your newfound knowledge of insects and the importance of protecting them, now is a great time to make them a shelter. Along with the odd bee, ladybirds and woodlice, you may even attract hedgehogs and toads. Autumn is an ideal time to make a wildlife hotel, as there will be plenty of dry grass, straw and hollow plant stems around. Research which creatures are attracted to different conditions; some, such as woodlice, like cooler, damper conditions and others, such as bees, prefer a warmer, sunnier location.

If you don't have your own garden, you could investigate public spaces and seek permission to build your wildlife hotel there. It may be a good thing to instigate in your local community garden, if there is one. Rope in some friends for a thoroughly edifying, bonding activity.

A SELECTION OF THINGS YOU COULD USE

- Old wooden pallets, and both strips and planks of wood
- Straw, moss, dry leaves and woodchips
- Old terracotta pots, old roof tiles and bricks with perforations
- Old logs, bark, pine cones, sand and soil
- Dead hollow stems (cut these from shrubs and herbaceous plants) and hollow bamboo canes
- A sheet of roofing felt
- Any other natural materials you find lying around in your garden and that are free to take

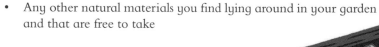

HOW TO CONSTRUCT

1. Ideally, your hotel should be no more than a metre in height.

2. Choose firm, level ground to build it on.

3. For a larger hotel, wooden pallets are ideal as they're sturdy and have gaps. The size of your hotel will depend on how much material you can gather.

4. Lay your bricks in an H shape, then add three or four layers of pallets on top.

5. When you're satisfied with the height, stabilise your construction with a roof made from old roof tiles or old planks, and cover with your roofing felt.

6. You want to create gaps, tunnels and beds, and fill them with creature-friendly materials. For beetles, woodlice and spiders, this means dead wood and bits of bark. For bees, this means small natural tubes made from bamboo and reeds. In the larger gaps and holes you could try bits of stone and tile for frogs and toads; this creates a warmer place for them to stay in winter, where they can feast on slugs. Dry leaves (which create the feel of a forest floor), thin branches and straw are good for aphid-eating ladybirds and beetles.

7. If your hotel is in a warm, sunny spot, plant nectar-rich flowers around it, such as sunflowers, comfrey and catmint, to attract bees.

8. Monitor your guests by visiting with a torch when it's cooler and darker; this is when activity is most likely to occur.

TAKE A TRAIN TRIP

In the autumn months, when the world outside is resplendent with colour, taking a trip to the countryside, the coast or to a nature reserve is a wonderful way of embracing the elements and experiencing the revitalising effects of an unfamiliar environment. Since the advent of cheap plane fares and the prevalence of cars, trains are mostly associated with commuting. It's true that trains can be expensive, and the journey can take longer, but if you choose the right time and route, train travel can offer spectacular views of the natural world, as well as a little romance, and the comfort of being carried along without the stress of driving or navigating a crowded airport. Trains are a great way of transporting us to nature as they provide a window-seat view of the stunning landscape all around us.

If you're on a budget, plan ahead and book an affordable return train ticket as soon as you can. There are lots of online resources and apps available to make sure you have the optimum train ride. Whether it's a simple train journey, a steam train excursion complete with afternoon tea, a romantic sleeper train or even a treat on the Orient Express, there are lots of options to choose from. It's a good idea to take layers of clothing, perhaps a neck pillow and some snacks and water for your journey. And if you want to take a pet with you, just remember to check that this is allowed on your particular journey.

VOLUNTEER ON AN ARABLE FARM

With our growing ecological and environmental awareness, learning about the origins and preparation of the plants we eat is a really useful way of broadening our knowledge about our food supply. Getting involved in harvesting crops at farms around the country is not only time well spent outdoors, it is also educational and great exercise. Farmers sometimes anticipate that their arable harvests will require extra hands to bring in, and though there is paid work available, becoming a volunteer from September to October is another excellent way of playing your part in the wider community. It will inspire a sense of purpose, and take you away from everyday stress to a world where the focus is on the here and now.

The good news is that you don't need a lot of experience to volunteer; a lot of farms will provide training, including on health and safety. You may need to have a certain level of fitness for the work involved, so couch potatoes (excuse the pun) may not want to apply, but enthusiasm, hard work and a developing appreciation of our agricultural world will go a long way. Start looking into volunteer work at farms in spring. If you are interested in working farther afield, you'll have to think about accommodation. Some farms provide this, but there is usually a fee to pay. If you haven't got the budget for that, then sticking to local farm opportunities is advisable.

CUDDLE WITH PIGS

Here are some essential pig facts.

1. Pigs only have a few sweat glands, which is why they love lounging around in cool mud.

2. The endearing grunts pigs make have a real purpose: to communicate with other pigs about their needs and the state of their health.

3. The pig's snout is a multi-functional organ, used for smelling out food, as well as digging for truffles. Their sense of smell is around two thousand times more powerful than ours.

4. They are highly sensual animals and love a good massage, rubbing themselves against trees and relaxing to music. Seriously.

5. They are highly social and affectionate and love to huddle and cuddle up with other pigs.

Pigs are recognised as mood-boosting companions. Mini, or micro-pigs, are often requested by schools to help children learn how to nurture animals, and at care homes for the elderly as a form of therapy for their residents. They're even used as an effective way to help university students relax and destress between exams.

Pigs are farm animals and are lawfully protected in Europe and the UK with certain rules. If you're thinking about being a permanent pig-owner, you'll need to abide by this legislation.

GUINEA PIG THERAPY

These domestic rodents have been a popular children's pet for decades, but the benefits they can provide for adult mental health are significant, too. Calmer and more docile than hamsters, guinea pigs are social creatures and many owners feel the same reciprocal loyalty with them as they do with dogs and cats. Their soft fur and bright, intelligent eyes make them pretty adorable, too. They also have a relatively long lifespan – up to seven years – so they'll be sticking around, if you take care of them.

If you're looking for a low-maintenance pet, giving a home to a guinea pig is worth considering. For those people who have limited mobility, these sweet creatures won't demand daily walks, just comfortable living conditions and affection. They're wonderful little companions, enabling important sensory touch, and will help to combat loneliness, depression, anxiety and stress.

You'll need to make sure you have no allergies associated with these pets, and that you are able to provide them with what they need. Most importantly, find one from a recommended and verified source.

PINE CONE BOWLING

Pine cones are one of autumn's most recognisable symbols. Around September, we start to see them scattered underneath conifer trees in our parks, forests and gardens. Before they drop, the cones are important as protective cases for pine seeds; their rounded scales keep the seeds safe from predators looking for a snack, ensuring new tree growth for the future. Pine cones are so pleasing to look at and so beautifully designed, it's almost as though they have been carved by hand, but they're just one more example of nature's extraordinary capacity for great design. Feeling the texture and shape of a pine cone can calm and destress us, even if we are not aware of it. Pine cones are functional, sensory and ornamental and they make delightful natural bowling pins or boules balls.

You'll need to set out for a good pine cone forage: try and gather at least 12 of similar size and shape. You can even spray paint the cones to distinguish them for each player. Then, armed with your boules or bowling rules, spend some time in your nearest green space enjoying a restful game. Pine cone bowling has been popular as a game for children for a long time, but it's a marvellous way of connecting with nature at any age.

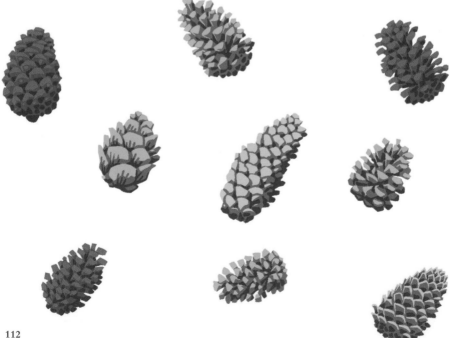

CREATE AN AUTUMN MOOD JOURNAL

As you journey through autumn, a great way of measuring its effect on your mental wellbeing is to keep a mood journal. Don't be surprised if your moods fluctuate regularly. We all have good days and bad days, but you may well discover that the weather, the temperature, your level of activity and how much time you have spent outdoors embracing nature can have a significant impact on how energetic, positive or stable your feelings are. Colour is important, too. When the days are overcast and dark, colour fades and often our mood fades along with it. Noticing how a cloudy, grey sky might make us lethargic, restless or generally low is a positive action, reminding us that these feelings are almost always temporary, as well as how much the natural world influences us. We are intimately connected with our surroundings, and the highs and lows we experience are all part of nature's process. Feeling this bond through the light and shade of our emotions strengthens and stabilises us, decreasing anxiety and feelings of foreboding.

You can keep a mood journal in a simple notebook, recording your feelings daily or weekly. You could also incorporate your journal in your Instagram feed, combining a visual record of the colours and sights outdoors with a mood caption. If you choose the latter, you'll inspire others, too.

PING PONG

Table tennis, or ping pong, is easy to learn and has an
abundance of mental agility and health benefits. It can be
played all year round, but a game outside on a crisp, autumn day warms you up
and boosts energy levels. It's guaranteed to have you laughing, even if your will to
win doesn't kick in.

Studies suggest that ping pong improves memory function and capacity to
concentrate for all ages, improving our cognitive ability and motor learning (our
ability to develop skills through practice). Some scientists believe the quick, rapid
movement required is a contributing factor. Like tennis and chess, ping pong is a
strategic game; players literally think on their feet, having to make decisions quickly.
It's also a social game, during which there is little or no room for anxious thoughts
because we are compelled to stay in each second and not project our minds any
further forward than our next move.

If you have a big enough garden or outside space, this will be an ideal place to set
up your table. All the necessary equipment can be bought fairly inexpensively, but
many urban parks have permanent ping pong tables; all you'll need is paddles and
balls. You can also improvise with an old kitchen table and a net.

FLY A KITE

Not surprisingly, kite-flying is considered one
of the best forms of all-round exercise, combining
low-impact aerobic movement with stretching,
improving heart health and agility. It is also excellent
as a mood-boosting activity and a brilliant way
of combining nature with sport. The kites are at the
mercy of the elements as they are carried through the
air, swooping and diving with the wind. Although March
can be a great time to take out a kite, the blustery days of
autumn are just as good.

As with table tennis, there's no need to master kite-flying
immediately (or at all). Although some people make their own
kites, it's less stressful to buy one from an accredited, verified source,
where you'll get advice on which kite is best for you. Your kite
needs three basic elements in order to be properly functional: the
correct aerodynamic structure to gain lift from the wind, a sturdy
tether to keep it blowing away and a good bridle that ensures
the kite is facing the wind at the right angle. Kites come in many
different shapes, sizes and colours, and at many different prices, so
you'll have plenty of options.

Get involved in the world of kite-flying, and a windy autumn
afternoon outside is transformed. With practice, you can learn to
choreograph aerial manoeuvres such as loops, backflips and
stalls, or you could keep it simple and just see how high
you can fly your kite.

FORAGE FOR AUTUMN DÉCOR

So many wonderful plants, flowers and berries can be found in the autumn: rich reds and greens among the golden-brown leaves and the fallen branches that scatter over the ground. This is a season that lends itself very well to creating home décor and you can craft a vivid natural environment inside your home when the temperatures dip outside. Bits of kindling, thin branches and autumn leaves all make wonderful decoration above fireplaces, or on shelves or tables.

When you set out for a walk to a park or wood, take a pair of secateurs with you ready to take cuttings. Keep your eyes peeled for 'old man's beard', also known as *Clematis vitalba*, which can be found early on in the season in mid to late September. Its flowering seeds present as long, silky tufts of hair, which you can adapt for your home by removing the seeds and using hairspray to help those glorious beards last. Then there are gorgeous rose hips – keep an eye out for round, pumpkin-shaped *Rosa rugosa* hips and star-shaped clusters of this flower. These need to be stored in a dark, dry area to keep the hips from shrivelling, as does hawthorn, once it has been cut into lengths and had its leaves removed. Spindle berries, with their pinkish-red foliage and bright orange seeds, are also a great find, as are hydrangeas, certain grasses and, later in the season, dogwood, eucalyptus, yew and fir. And we mustn't forget about those traditional autumn-winter favourites, holly and mistletoe.

PRESERVING BERRIES AND FLOWERS

Household glycerine is excellent for keeping the colour and softer texture of flowers and berries alive for longer in your home, as it prevents them from drying out. You can buy glycerine from any chemist. Here's how to preserve berries and flowers.

1. First, leave the stems of your plants in water for around eight hours, to hydrate them.

2. Cut a little off your stems and carefully crush the ends with your fingers.

3. Now fill a glass jar (a jam jar is perfect) with about a centimetre of glycerine and a couple of centimetres of hot water (filtered if possible).

4. Leave your stems in this glycerine-water mix for as long as it takes for the liquid to absorb into your stems. This can take around two weeks.

5. Position your newly-revived cuttings as table centrepieces, mantelpiece features or bedroom or windowsill decoration.

For more information on what plant life to look for in autumn, visit trusted online resources, such as The Woodland Trust.

PUMPKIN PICKING

Another vivid symbol of autumn, the pumpkin has its moment in the spotlight from mid to late October – though pumpkins can be picked for seven or eight weeks and they are much more than Halloween motifs.

If you have the space, you can grow your own pumpkins. They're pretty low maintenance and are best started off from seeds indoors around April, then moved outside to catch the sun in summer, before being harvested in the autumn. But there's also a lot to be said for pumpkin picking at local farms in both urban and rural areas, and many city farms have pumpkin patches. So, make a note in your diary to visit a nearby patch around mid to late October. You'll probably need to book as demand is high. And remember, pumpkins are heavy, so you'll need to consider how you'll transport them back home.

PUMPKIN POWER

Carving pumpkins to make Halloween lanterns is always fun. You'll need the right utensils: a large, sturdy, serrated kitchen knife for major carving, along with a paring knife for more delicate craftsmanship, and an ice-cream scoop for gouging out the flesh (you can keep the flesh to cook with later). You might want to paint your pumpkins, so use acrylic or spray paint, which won't crack on the pumpkin's skin. And they'll look amazing with an LED tealight positioned inside.

SPICED PUMPKIN BUTTER

Delicious spread on toast, crumpets and pancakes, this is a healthy autumnal treat. You'll need:

- Around 850 g (2 x 425 g tins) of pumpkin puree (or make your own by peeling and seeding the fruit, cutting into cubes, then steaming for 10 to 15 minutes until soft)
- 120 ml of apple juice
- 2 tsp of ground ginger
- 1 tsp of ground cinnamon
- 250 ml of maple syrup
- a small nutmeg for grating
- 2 tsp of vanilla paste

COOKING

1. Combine all your ingredients in a pan, add a pinch of salt, then put the pan on a medium heat and bring to the boil.

2. Now reduce the heat to simmer for between 20 to 30 minutes, stirring regularly.

3. You'll know your butter is cooked when it's thickened and is a lovely golden-brown colour.

4. Empty your cooked mixture into a bowl and leave to cool completely, then scoop into clean containers (glass jars are best) and keep in the fridge for up to a week.

VISIT A HISTORIC HOUSE AND GROUNDS

Taking a day trip to a historic house or stately home is a wonderful experience – a visual and sensory history lesson with a touch of old-fashioned glamour. In the UK, you can walk in the footsteps of aristocracy, exploring opulent buildings and enjoying beautiful landscaped gardens and expansive estates. Some of these heritage homes are embedded in acres of countryside. Others, such as London's Kenwood House, or the beautiful Eltham Palace, are in cities. These and many other architectural portals to the past are found all around the UK and in Europe, each of them uniquely enchanting, with its own historical attractions.

Historic houses and their grounds are open to the public most of the year, but check whether you need to book in advance before you go. You usually have to pay an entrance fee or make a donation. You may want to check what the weather conditions are like for the day of your visit, though even when it's cold and rainy, a wander through beautiful grounds can be magical.

ESCAPE TO A NATIONAL PARK

The creation of Britain's national parks was at least partly inspired by the country's early 19th-century poets, Lord Byron, Samuel Taylor Coleridge and William Wordsworth. They were all passionate about the beauty of the natural world, influencing the public to demand greater access to it. Thanks to them, there are now over a dozen of these carefully maintained natural breathing spaces in the UK, providing acres of lovingly treated land for all kinds of plants and wildlife. Between them, these parks have paid host to hundreds of conservation projects, where nature is protected and people can improve their wellbeing.

For a breathtaking natural experience, there's little to beat a national park. Combining stunning landscapes and wildlife with geographical heritage, your park visit will be unique and unforgettable. From scenic waterways and mudflats to ancient trees, grazing wildlife, mountains and lakes, you'll find a perfect nature experience wherever you are in the country. Respect for nature is vital, so make sure you research what you'll need before you go, any rules and regulations, opening times and entrance fees, then prepare for a spectacular experience.

COMMUNITY CARING OUTSIDE

While you're strengthening your own mental wellbeing with more time spent out in nature, consider helping more vulnerable members of the community do the same. Depending on how fragile or buoyant you're feeling, you may not feel able to look after others as well as yourself, and that is perfectly OK. But if you feel up to it, the benefits to those you're helping, as well as the emotional reward you'll receive for your efforts, are considerable. For the elderly living on their own, some company, a chat and an adventure outdoors can be a lifeline. Studies have shown that fresh air, regular exercise and mentally stimulating activities really boost the elderly's quality of life and help combat the loneliness that arises when they are separated from their loved ones. And the experience isn't one-way, either; there's a lot to learn from older generations. Spend some time listening to their stories and you'll gain a new perspective, and perhaps a new friend. The start of autumn can be an unsettling time for the vulnerable, as it limits their options, so it's an ideal time for this activity.

HOW TO HELP

- If you know any lonely elderly people living locally to you and who still have independence, along with making an effort to telephone or visit them weekly for a catch-up, take them out for a walk! Helping a lonely or immobile person take a stroll outside can help combat loneliness as well as providing the usual benefits of time spent in nature.

- Depending on their physical capabilities, you could encourage your new friend(s) to help you garden. They may well have a thing or two to teach you about horticulture!

- Engage in a little light outdoor ping pong, and make sure to build in rests, during which you could play a board game to pass the time.

- Most importantly of all, listen to what their interests are and choose activities accordingly.

- You can also volunteer for organisations that support older people – there are lots of established ones. They can instigate befriending programmes for the more isolate elderly, and welcome 'active buddies' who can have one-to-one contact with them, accompanying them outside for walks, or driving them to the seaside for an afternoon.

- When you are out and about, be kind. Let the elderly or more vulnerable members of society know they are seen. Smile, wave, even stop and chat if it feels appropriate. It could be the difference between a good day and bad day for both of you.

BECOME A RAMBLER

If you're sociable and thrive on being active while getting to know new people, rambling could be the perfect outdoor activity for you. Ramblers come in all shapes, sizes and ages, and the popularity of this group pursuit is increasing. Many people find that a Saturday or Sunday spent heading out to beautiful countryside to embark on a few hours walking, stopping off for refreshments along the way, is a wonderful antidote to stressful weekly lives and preferable to socialising in pubs and restaurants. You'll end your ramble feeling both invigorated and tired, in the best possible way. You'll sleep better, feel calmer and enjoy the buzz of being part of a team. You do generally have to be over 18, and be responsible about your own state of health. If you have any underlying health conditions, you must first ask a medical expert if rambling is suitable for you.

Once you decide to go for it, contact the various rambling organisations to find out how you enrol, what sorts of routes are available and which are best for you and what you need to wear and bring with you. You'll see some spectacular natural sights in all weathers, and the wider perspective you'll gain on our world and its idiosyncratic beauty is priceless.

JOIN IN WITH A PARK WALK

Park walks are a wonderful activity for the elderly, stimulating good physical health and providing fresh air and companionship. All different levels of physical fitness are accommodated, too. But you don't need to be a senior citizen to get involved in a park walk. For younger folk, a hearty walk around their local park with like-minded people can be an excellent alternative to running or jogging, which is tougher on our joints and muscles and more likely to cause injuries. Also, some people just don't like running (fair enough!) and prefer the lower impact, sociable nature of a good brisk walk. Any exercise done in slightly cooler weather is more comfortable as you'll heat up as you go, so this is an activity for spring/early summer or autumn, or the less harsh periods of winter. If this sounds appealing, here's how to prepare:

- If you're thinking this will be a regular activity, you'll need to invest in some strong, comfortable and durable footwear. Something between a trainer and a mountain-hiking boot is about right, but we're all different so consult with experts online or in specialist shops.

- Wear cotton layers on top to keep you warm and to allow ventilation, and comfortable joggers or leggings. For outerwear, choose lightweight, rainproof jackets that won't weigh you down but will keep the rain off and the wind out.

- Be realistic about your walking speed. Though walking briskly is good for our cardiac health, any walking is good. A park walk is about more than fitness – it's about companionship and engagement with nature.

PREPARING FOR
DARKER MONTHS

We've talked about how the changing seasons affect us — how low in energy and anxious we can feel during the transition. As autumn draws to a close and the bright, hot summer seems light years away, it is typically more of a challenge for us to sustain mental wellbeing as we cross over into the darkest, coldest months of the year. If we were squirrels, we would be foraging for food to tuck away to last us through the harsh winter period; these innovative creatures, like many animals (and plantlife), instinctively know how to move through one season to another. And though the needs of the animal kingdom are based on basic survival, we could learn a thing or two from their habits. Now is the time to employ some useful techniques and practise self-care.

If you have been keeping a visual or written journal on each season and its effects on your wellbeing, make a note to continue this going forward. As December approaches, make sure you capture as many of nature's changes as you can. The world changes quickly at this time of year, and if you concentrate on wonder and fascination, rather than mourning the loss of the summer, it can help you to see this period in a more positive light. It can serve as a reminder of the transience of all living things, which are in perpetual motion, moving forward — because that's the only direction there is. Once you embrace this natural way of being, and remind yourself that all our emotions are important and shouldn't be feared, you will move into the new season with strength.

WAYS TO PREPARE FOR CHANGE

1. Think practically and make sure all your domestic needs are catered to for the winter. Fix any insulation issues with your home and ensure you have enough warm clothes to see you through the season.

2. Stock up on food rich in vitamins and minerals, which will help keep you healthy during the winter. Carrots contain vitamin C, an important antioxidant that helps your body produce collagen. Beetroot helps your body eliminate toxins. Spinach, kale and cabbage all contain vitamin K, which is excellent for skin maintenance, and broccoli is packed full of vitamins and minerals and antioxidants, too.

3. Be good to your body – take the time to exfoliate, practice circulation-boosting exercises such as a brisk walk or a run and focus on core strengthening exercises like pilates and yoga.

4. Get plenty of sleep. Early dinners, early nights and early mornings are wonderful for maintaining energy.

5. Make plans with your friends for the months ahead. Isolation is a key factor in depression and anxiety, and having social events to look forward to keeps you feeling part of your community.

WINTER

STARGAZING

We know how beautiful a clear night sky is when
it's dotted with stars, whether it's a perfect, late summer
evening, or a crisp winter's night. Some studies have shown that
stargazing is not only good for your mental and emotional wellbeing, bringing
calm after the stresses of everyday life, it can actually make us nicer people! Whether
you have a hectic job that leaves you a little drained at the end of each day, or
you've spent the day cooking, cleaning or caring for children, taking the time to sit
outside after dark on a cloudless night and look up at nature's spectacular night-
time canopy brings instant perspective.

The sky is a kind of doorway to infinite Space and, contemplating this, we start to
feel humbled. Each of us is important individually, of course, but we are also all part
of a vast universe. Remembering this, as we turn our faces up to the sky, reminds us
that we are part of the collective human race, each of us bringing something unique
to life on Earth. For a brief time, we can let go of the need to control what happens
in our lives. Stargazing encourages acceptance and a community spirit – it quite
literally helps us see the bigger picture.

Another great reason to stargaze is to encourage our creativity. Our creative brain
is triggered when we allow ourselves the mental space to let our ideas come. During
the day, as we go about our everyday tasks and responsibilities, our minds are
whirring with thoughts and anxiety, and the pressure of this leaves very little space
in our brains for anything else. There is simply no time to be creative! Stopping and
allowing our thoughts to slow down encourages our imagination to unfold . . .

TOP TIPS FOR STARGAZING

1. First, do some research online. Find out what stars you can view and the best time to view them. There are also impressive astro apps available that you can download to your phone. They can map your location and guide you through your stargazing experience.

2. Stargazing is best done when the sky is cold, clear and crisp, not humid, so you'll need to wrap up warm and perhaps take a hot drink with you. Ideally, choose a night when there's a new moon or a crescent moon; a full moon will produce too much light and diminish the appearance of the surrounding stars.

3. If you're a city dweller, find a spot high up, so that buildings and unnatural light don't impede your view of the sky. If it's really dark and you need to take a torch, a torch with a red filter is better for your eyes and optimal vision. If you're using your phone as your torch, make your own red filter by covering your phone with translucent red paper.

4. You don't need fancy equipment to get to know the night sky. Start by learning to identify planets, stars and constellations with just the naked eye. For the more advanced stargazer, a telescope and binoculars will magnify your view and heighten the experience, but neither are necessary when it comes to your enjoyment and sense of connection with the celestial bodies surrounding Planet Earth.

MAKE A HOLIDAY WREATH

Kicking this dramatic season off by creating a wonderful winter wreath is a great way of channelling our creativity. It's also a great excuse to get outside and hunt for natural materials. Having a goal that encourages us to venture outside helps us adapt to and embrace the winter environment, and see the beauty in nature's cycle. The origins of the wreath date back to Ancient Roman, Egyptian and Greek times – for these civilisations, it was a symbol of victory, power and everlasting life. Traditionally, wreaths are made from evergreens: holly, ivy, yew, eucalyptus and pine foliage. These plants are resilient and enduring, and represent eternal life and stamina. Keep this symbolism in mind as an affirmation of your own resilience and strength.

Decide whether your wreath will be an outdoor or indoor one. Outdoor wreaths usually last five to six weeks and those hung indoors last around two weeks, so timing your forage is important. Although evergreen foliage and berries make for a greener wreath, you can also use dogwood, willow, hazel or birch for a more rustic look. Make sure you gather plenty of foliage – more than you think you'll need – and look out for holly, cotoneaster or ivy berries to add colour.

WHAT YOU'LL NEED FOR YOUR WREATH

This guide is for a simple eucalyptus wreath, which dries out well and smells wonderful. For more wreath ideas, consult a crafts website or an online video tutorial. You'll need:

- Secateurs for cutting your leaves and berries

- A copper ring or gardening wire of at least 10 inches or a wooden embroidery hoop

- Craft wire or florist's wire

- Scissors

- Conifer twigs

- Mixed eucalyptus (you can use dried, but fresh is better for more flexible stems), and berries (see page 117 for berries preserved in glycerine, which will last longer)

CREATION

1. Starting on the left, lay your conifer twigs face up around your ring, covering about two thirds of the ring itself.

2. Now cut small pieces of wire and use them to carefully attach the conifers to your ring.

3. Lay your eucalyptus stems over your conifers, cut to a length of around twelve inches. Attach them with wire, then add another layer – try and mix up the different kinds of eucalyptus.

4. Now thread in your berries, embedding them in the eucalyptus and using wire again to make sure to attach them to the ring.

You can display your wreath indoors – on a door (if it has a hook), or mount it on a mantelpeice – and bring winter's fresh natural materials inside. You can also hang it from your door knocker so that others can enjoy it outside.

TECH HABITS TO
LIFT YOUR MOOD

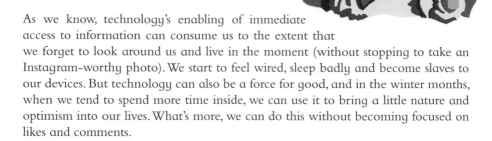

As we know, technology's enabling of immediate
access to information can consume us to the extent that
we forget to look around us and live in the moment (without stopping to take an
Instagram-worthy photo). We start to feel wired, sleep badly and become slaves to
our devices. But technology can also be a force for good, and in the winter months,
when we tend to spend more time inside, we can use it to bring a little nature and
optimism into our lives. What's more, we can do this without becoming focused on
likes and comments.

Changing the wallpaper on your phone is a good place to start. Just switching it to
something bright, natural and joyful – perhaps a memory of a wonderful holiday or
outdoor adventure – reminds us that we can be transported by the sight of a beach
at dusk, a mountain piercing a bright blue sky, a vivid green forest or a tranquil
river. Darker days require brighter stimulation, and our visual sense is a hugely
powerful rescue remedy. You can then do the same on your computer, and with any
screensavers.

Keeping nature and its wonderfully soothing effects in mind, start following social
media accounts that celebrate the beautiful outdoors, wildflowers and wildlife, or
accounts that champion action against climate change and animal extinction. Be
inspired by your tech in ways that don't play into any insecurities or anxiety you
might be prone to. By learning more about our natural world, its beauty
and any threat to it, and doing whatever we can to keep it
thriving, we are reminded that we are each part of
a global community and that taking
care of the Earth means
we are taking care
of ourselves.

VISIT A DRAMATIC LANDSCAPE

Winter is a dramatic season, as it's a time when the elements can be at their most extreme. Bitter cold, rain, snow and strong blustery winds are often considered problematic. But if we can appreciate nature's theatrics and develop wonder instead of discontent, our nervous systems will calm as we stop fighting with, and start embracing, our environment.

To help you embrace winter, think about visiting a dramatic landscape. There is hardly a country in the world that doesn't offer spectacular, unforgettable terrain. In the UK, dramatic gems include the Lake District, with its snow-capped mountains towering above tranquil stretches of water, where goats graze in surrounding fields, or the clifftops of the very tip of Cornwall at Land's End; here, majestic waves crash against the shore and rise up the craggy cliffs. And Scotland has some of the most beautiful scenery in the world, with its remote isles and cottages, its gorse-strewn hills and mountains, and its famous lochs. Wherever you live, a dramatic landscape is often only a train trip away. Visiting somewhere unfamiliar will make your experience more impactful, too. Make sure it's safe to visit, that you have the right apparel and some emergency supplies of food and water in case you don't encounter a café or shop along the way.

MOSS SPOTTING

Moss – the modest, springy, green plant that sprawls over rocks and stones, embeds itself in our pathways and carpets woodlands – is all around us. We may not give it much thought, but moss is an important contributor to the health of our ecosystem and one of the first colonisers of bare ground. It absorbs large amounts of water, soaking up rainfall and producing a locally humid environment. It also serves as a home for the likes of woodlice and slugs – though birds are often wise to this and use their beaks to dig moss up looking for a tasty invertebrate meal.

Moss also has a beneficial effect on our senses and our emotional state. Colour-therapy studies show that the colour green promotes feelings of good health, harmony and balance within us – no surprise, then, that the abundance of green in nature can transform our mood. If you're not up for keeping indoor plants, moss is a fabulous alternative when it comes to filling your home with green stuff. Originally popular in Japan, moss balls will give a table decoration a tranquil, natural feel when arranged in a shallow dish. And a moss wreath made of different varieties has a pretty, otherworldly appearance. Moss's tactile nature makes it particularly pleasing, so investigate some moss crafts and see what you can make from moss you spot on a walk. You'll be surprised at how many varieties there are!

The most common kinds of moss can be found in woodland, by streams and rivers or growing on tree stumps. One variety, common haircap moss, resembles a miniature pine forest, can grow up to 40 cm tall and is found in more acidic areas of land like bogs, wet heaths and moorland. And silky forklet moss is characterised by thin, yellow-green leaves, curled in the same direction, forming clumps about 3 cm tall. This can be seen in more shaded areas such as ditches, banks and woodland, and it loves acidic soil. Other kinds of moss include swan's neck thyme moss, common tamarisk moss, glittering wood moss (so called because of its glossy leaves) and springy turf moss (the kind we see on our garden paths). Mosses thrive in winter weather, so this is an excellent time to become a moss expert. Take a checklist of the different varieties and spend a day photo-journalling your discoveries.

WANDER THROUGH A PINE FOREST

Pine trees are closely associated with winter, mostly because fir trees are associated with Christmas. Live pine trees are evergreen, which means unlike many other tree species they keep their needles all year round, and this makes pine forests a spectacular sight. Seen from above, they are a glorious sweep of bottle green, often running up and down hilly areas. And taking a walk through a pine forest makes for a fairy-tale experience. All varieties of pine give off a fresh, camphor-like scent that enables us to breathe more deeply, pumping oxygen into our lungs and up to our brains. Its psychological effects are important, too. Pine is a rejuvenator for body and mind, boosting our energy levels and our spirits.

Spending time in a pine forest in winter, when we may be feeling more mentally and physically fragile, can be a wonderfully restorative experience. Find your nearest area of pine trees, and put a note in your winter diary for some invaluable pine therapy. You could also take a bag out with you and collect some of the fallen pine cones you'll spot on your walk; along with pine cone bowling (see page 112), getting creative with pine cones will make for some fabulous home décor!

SURF'S UP!

We usually associate surfing with
bright Californian or Australian beaches,
where golden-skinned fitties effortlessly ride the waves on hot summer days, but
winter surfing is every bit as exhilarating, and even better for our mental health.
Latest studies reveal that one of the reasons winter surfing has such a beneficial
effect on our mental health is that the colder the water, the more our sympathetic
(fight or flight) and parasympathetic (calm) nervous systems are stimulated. Our
vagus nerve, which regulates our internal organ functions such as digestion, heart
function and respiratory rate, is also stimulated. Simply put, we function at a high
level when we winter surf, and it has been known to decrease symptoms of epilepsy,
as well as to significantly reduce anxiety and stress.

If you're shivering at the thought of it, be reassured that while your mind and
body are reaping the rewards of this cold-water exercise, you'll have a wetsuit to
protect you from adverse effects of the water's temperature. You don't need to be
an Olympic-level surfer, though you will need to be a proficient swimmer. You will
also need to seek proper tuition from a qualified surf instructor, as well as declare
any underlying health conditions to health professional before you start. If you're
already a summer surfer, then you'll have a bit of a headstart, but there are still some
important differences to bear in mind.

PREPARING FOR YOUR WINTER SURF

1. If you don't have your own surfboard, most surf beaches hire them out. Seek advice about the best board for your size and level of skill.

2. A well-fitting wetsuit is vital. Ask expert advice on what kind of thickness is best for winter temperatures. Wetsuits come in a variety of thicknesses, with fleeced lining and, ideally, liquid seams.

3. Your head, hands and feet need insulation, too: a hat, gloves and boots are essential.

4. Make sure your kit is ready to put on as soon as you arrive at the beach. Putting everything in an open basket, rather than a rucksack or holdall, means it's more accessible and can be put on quickly. Bring a towelling robe with you to help keep you warm when you get out.

5. It's vital that you're not too cold or too warm before you get in the water. If you're too cold, you won't be able to heat up once you're in the water. If you're changing outside in winter, it's a good idea to wear a padded coat and put your suit on underneath it. If you're changing inside, do it in an unheated room, otherwise the shock of the cold will be greater when you get into the sea.

6. You should always surf with at least one friend; it's safer, and it's more enjoyable.

7. When you're in the water, take notice of what your body is telling you. When you're paddling, the activity will generate body heat, but when you stop, your body starts to cool. If you are inactive for too long, your extremities will become numb and you could be at risk from hypothermia. A shorter, active session is easier on your body than a longer period with less movement. Don't hang around in the water: get out as soon as you're done.

8. Time is of the essence when you emerge from your surf. Make sure your robe and your clothes are ready and accessible for you to put on as quickly as possible. An insulated beanie hat is a must for your head. Make sure you've brought a flask with a hot drink, too; it'll warm you up instantly.

PURIFY YOUR HOME

In winter, we naturally spend more time inside, with
the central heating and the oven on more often, and
this means the air in our homes can get stuffy. Throwing
open a window is one solution, though colder outside
temperatures make it an undesirable and short-lived one.
Another great option is to get some air purifying plants.
Through photosynthesis, these plants not only convert the
carbon dioxide we breathe out into fresh oxygen, they also help
remove toxins, which can linger indoors, from the air we are breathing in.

The pretty 'eternity plant' is ideal for purifying-plant novices as it needs little light,
can manage for over a week without water and doesn't attract insects. If you have
a pet, though, it's a no-no as it can be toxic to animals. An erstwhile favourite, the
spider plant is a great all-rounder; it looks distinctive, is low maintenance and pet-
friendly. If you're looking for something a little different, the parlor palm will give
your home a touch of summer, as it's essentially a miniature palm tree. Though it
looks delicate, the parlor palm is pretty resilient, can sit in darker parts of the house
and isn't harmful to animals. All it requires is a spritz of water on its leaves every
few days. There's also the popular philodendron, which comes in several varieties, is
lovely to look at and likes a dry atmosphere. If you have children or pets, it can be
dangerous as the leaves are poisonous if ingested. You'll also need to make sure you
don't over-hydrate this plant as it absorbs water slowly. There are lots more plants
to consider, but be sure to seek expert advice if you're in
doubt about a plant's safety. Once you've made your
choice and positioned it in your home, make sure
you turn it regularly towards the sunlight, even if it
doesn't need much.

BRING ESSENTIAL
OILS INTO YOUR LIFE

Essential oils are not only a wonderful sensory experience, they genuinely improve our wellbeing through their plant origins. We've talked about the power of lavender (see page 66), which smells divine and can have many positive effects on the human body, including slowing the heart rate and calming the nervous system. But there are many other deliciously scented plant oils available to make your home a restful and aromatic place to be.

Mandarin, bergamot and ylang-ylang are sweetly scented, can ease anxiety and help you sleep. You can also try peppermint or tea-tree oil, both of which ease stress and are marvellous, fresh-smelling natural decongestants, making them ideal for winter. Make sure you steer clear of using candles to heat up your oils in the bedroom; any candle left unattended presents a fire risk and your oil's effects may take a little while to permeate a room. Instead, use a room diffuser or spray them on your pillow.

For your living room, electric oil diffusers are good options. Diffusers come in a variety of shapes and sizes and work by gently boiling oil-infused water to give off aromatic steam. In your bathroom, use a reed diffuser to scent the room, or add your essential oils to carrier oils such as coconut and jojoba, so they can be safely added to your bath.

Make sure you are clear on which oils are safe to use. Some plants, even though they're organic, can contain materials that are toxic or cause skin irritation. Be very wary of buying any that are not proven to be safe, whether generally or for you specifically (particularly if you are adding drops to a bath). Take your time choosing the right oils and scents for you. If possible, sample them before you buy. Now relax and enjoy a wonderfully pampering experience.

CHASE A STORM

Storm-chasing has been a mental-health pursuit since the 19th century, practised with the goal of attaining a visceral connection to nature. The theory is that by walking towards and not away from extreme meterological conditions, we heighten our engagement with natural forces, gain more mental focus and relinquish the control we cling to that often only makes us feel more stressed. In 1874 one notable storm chaser, John Muir, climbed to the top of a 100-foot spruce tree during a wild storm in Sierra, California, and clung there for hours until the storm subsided. He wrote of his experience, 'Never before did I enjoy so noble an exhilaration of motion.' Serious storm chasers have described it as 'peak experience', giving them a profound understanding of their place in the universe – and 'a beautiful, cosmic moment'.

For most of us, the thought of facing extreme weather is understandably daunting, and we don't need to put ourselves in any danger to reap the benefits that come from storm-chasing. Taking a walk in windy conditions or through a light snow storm can be magical – a wonderfully bracing and humbling experience. It is also a valuable reminder that we cannot control everything around us, and that developing acceptance of the literal and metaphorical storms that arise in our lives is important for decreasing fear and anxiety and increasing mental strength and resilience. Make sure you have a tracking device on your phone to avoid getting lost, then relax and enjoy your wander.

PREPARING FOR A WINTER WONDERLAND WALK

There's an old saying, 'there's no such as thing as bad weather, only inappropriate clothes', so before embracing the elements, make sure you have the right gear.

1. Don't wear cotton or denim, which quickly absorb water and will stay wet, making you much colder if you are out in snow or rain. Instead, wear layers of man-made fabrics or silk.

2. For your base layer, material such as polyester wick moisture away from your skin and keep you from getting clammy. The next layer should be a top that you can easily take off if you get too hot – something fleecy or made of wool is great. Then you'll need an insulating layer, such as a quilted down or polyester microfleece vest or waistcoat. These will be more effective than an extra jacket underneath your final outerlayer.

3. For your outerlayer, a rainproof, windproof, breathable jacket made from a material such as Gore-tex is ideal.

4. For really cold conditions, consider wearing tights under your trousers to keep you cosy – tights made of silk or polypropylene are great.

5. Flexible trousers are a must: running leggings or tracksuit bottoms made of wicking polyester fabric are ideal. You could also invest in some waterproof, fleece-lined trousers, which will keep you dry and warm.

6. You can buy socks combining wicking polypropylene and wool layers from specialist shops, and they're worth investing in. Make sure they're not so thick that you can't put your boots on, though!

7. You'll need flexible, athletic footwear that's waterproof and windproof. A lightweight hiking boot or trail running shoe could also work. Seek expert advice if you're in any doubt.

8. Finally, don't forget a fleece-lined beanie hat to cover your ears and thermal gloves to keep your hands warm. And a wool or fleece scarf or snood will keep your neck cosy.

LET'S GO TRIG BAGGING

Trig pillars were once used for Ordnance Survey mapping of geographical points on high ground around the country, though they've now been replaced by GPS. You may well have seen these stone monuments without knowing what they are. Trig bagging – finding and checking off these pillars wherever they are – is an increasingly popular pastime, combining exercise with a satisfying mission. Trig baggers are serious about their hobby; it takes them all over the country and offers a slice of history. And just like pillboxes, the concrete pillars have an almost ghostly presence, standing abandoned on lonely hilltops. For those of us who like to attach a purpose to our outdoor experience and enjoy a challenge, trig bagging could be just the thing. And there are plenty of them in the UK: 6190, to be precise. That should keep you busy. Here are some tips to help you prepare.

1. Set yourself a goal to find a certain number of pillars over the winter months. Look for pillars that are within a reasonable/accessible distance. Once you've got that information, think about ways you could combine your pillar search with a weekend walking adventure.

2. If you can, download the Ordnance Survey map on your phone; it's important for GPS location tracking. There are dedicated trig-bagging websites that will guide you to apps that specifically map trig pillars. If you can't get online easily (or at all) while you're out, a physical Ordnance Survey map is a must.

3. You may have to travel by car or train to reach some pillars, but make sure you allow for as much walking as possible.

4. Prepare for the weather, and for remote countryside with no shops for miles. This means layered, windproof and rainproof clothing, footwear fit for hilly terrain and supplies of food and water.

VISIT A CITY FARM

This is one for city dwellers who may have limited time, a tight budget and no outside space, but who are passionate about animals. You'll find city farms in many urban areas, and they are truly wonderful places to visit. They usually house a wide variety of animals, the likes of which you may only otherwise see if you make time to visit the countryside. A city farm accommodates animals like horses, goats, sheep and sometimes even llamas. Many of the farms run volunteer workshops, where you can muck in and learn how the farm is run and cares for its occupants, giving you the chance to get up close to cute bunnies or snorting piglets. City farms are oases of rural joy, practically on your doorstep. Here are a few things to consider before your visit.

1. If it's voluntary work you're after rather than a visit, be aware that you can't just turn up at a farm. Check out the proper procedure first by visiting your chosen farm's website. Volunteer workshops will almost certainly require an application process. If you're working with animals, the farm staff will need to know that you're ready to do so. Be prepared to be put on a waiting list, or to travel further afield to secure a place.

2. Consider whether you have any allergies that can be triggered by animals. If you do have an allergy, you can still visit, but you may have to keep your distance from the animals.

3. Dress in warm, layered clothing that you don't mind getting dirty. You'll need practical and comfortable footwear: wellies are ideal because you can wipe them down if they get muddy.

GET ENGAGED WITH BIODOMES

If you're passionate about our ecosystem and reducing chemical and pesticide use, then you'll find biodomes fascinating. Simply put, a biodome is a self-contained and self-sufficient environment for plant and animal nurturing and cultivation – it's a space that has no interaction with the outside world. Inside this large, usually spherical, super-powerful green house, plants and animals work naturally together to regenerate more life. It's literally a circle of life.

If you have the outside space, it's possible to build your very own mini biodome with a special kit. It's an ambitious undertaking, so it's not for the faint-hearted or for those who have limited time and budget. If you are willing and able to provide your own home-grown food, minus the chemical cocktails, and contribute to the health of the environment, it's a worthy undertaking. But don't worry if that's not possible – there are large biodomes all over the world that you can visit, including the Eden Project in Cornwall. The Eden Project is the world's largest rainforest in captivity, and a living example of regeneration and sustainability. It's set within 30 acres of stunning garden, with sculpture, art and cutting-edge architecture, as well as inspiring demonstrations on sustainability.

GO SLEDGING

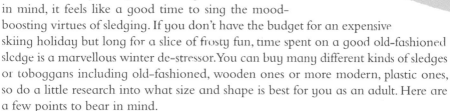

Some meteorological experts say that at the
current rate of global warming, within just a few
decades the snowfall we are used to seeing most
winters in Europe may cease altogether. With this
in mind, it feels like a good time to sing the mood-
boosting virtues of sledging. If you don't have the budget for an expensive
skiing holiday but long for a slice of frosty fun, time spent on a good old-fashioned
sledge is a marvellous winter de-stressor. You can buy many different kinds of sledges
or toboggans including old-fashioned, wooden ones or more modern, plastic ones,
so do a little research into what size and shape is best for you as an adult. Here are
a few points to bear in mind.

1. If you have any underlying health conditions, including osteoporosis, then you
   must seek medical advice first.

2. It's vital to dress for the snow and ice – you'll need a hat, gloves, warm waterproof
   trousers and snow-friendly, rubber-soled boots if possible. Thermal underwear
   and layers made of polypropylene are advisable. Wear a snood rather than a
   scarf, which might get caught on a passing branch or under the runners.

3. It's important to protect your head, and a cycling helmet is perfect for this.

4. Make sure you apply sunscreen, some chapstick and wear sunglasses. The sun's
   rays can still be fierce in snowy conditions and the extreme cold will dry out
   your lips.

5. If you're sledging some distance from home or from a café, then bring a flask
   with a hot drink, and pop some snacks in a bag for when you finish sledging.

BATHS, SPAS AND SAUNAS

Showers are great. They're environmentally friendly, refreshing and time-efficient, and in general should be our go-to form of body-cleansing. But the health benefits of a good bath are plentiful. Though extremely hot baths can put a strain on the heart, a good steamy bath better enables oxygen intake, improves blood flow and lung function, clears sinuses, relieves joint or muscle pain and reduces inflammation by calming the nervous system – soothing anxiety and stress levels. On a basic level, bathing compels us to slow down and focus on the present, inducing a meditative state of mind. Quite simply, bathtime is an all-round, healing experience. To heighten your relaxation, add bath salts or essential oils to your bath water (see page 141). Consider time spent in the tub as an act of self-love and care!

If you're looking for a little more drama, an outdoor sauna in winter is a truly exhilarating experience. In Scandinavian culture, the 'sauna in the snow' ritual is a favourite part of the long, dark winter. It's a time to relax with family and friends and benefits us both physically and mentally, though a little courage is involved. The idea is to work up a sweat in the sauna, then, while your body is still hot, roll around in the snow for a thorough cleanse and exfoliation. You don't need to employ this extreme method to reap the reward of the hot-cold treatment, though. If you have the budget, research your nearest outdoor spa hotel or facility and consider booking yourself in for an experience that guarantees to press your reset button.

MAKE BEAUTIFUL BATH SALTS

Heighten your bathtime experience with your own customised, aromatic and relaxing bath salts. They're simple to make, requiring just salt, essential oils and baking soda.

1. You'll need a glass jar container (a clean jam jar will work well), some coarse sea salt, epsom salts, baking soda and essential oils. Try a few if you don't already have a favourite and turn to page 141 if you need more info.

2. For natural food colouring, collect winter rose petals, spread them in a single layer on a paper towel on a plate, cover them with more paper towel and pop them in the microwave for 45 to 60 seconds. This will draw the moisture from your petals. Leave them to cool for a few minutes.

3. In a large mixing bowl, combine 6 parts coarse sea salt to 3 parts epsom salts (these soothe tired muscles and ease inflammation) to one part baking soda (this will soften your bath water and helps with skin irritation). Now add a few drops of your essential oil.

4. Now, gently stir in your rose petals, distributing them as evenly as you can through your salt-oils mixture. You'll start to inhale the delicious fresh scent quite quickly.

5. Put the lid on your container, label it and leave for few hours to settle.

6. Enjoy!

CELEBRATE THE WINTER SOLSTICE

It can be hard to feel inspired by the dark days of winter, though it might be some comfort to know that the winter blues have been a common issue for millennia. In Greek mythology, Persephone (daughter of the god, Zeus) was banished to the underworld for the winter season, and Shakespeare wrote, 'a sad tale's best for winter'. The winter solstice, however, is a cause for celebration, marking the end of shorter, dark days and the beginning of our journey to spring. It happens in the same 24-hour period in December around the world. In the Northern Hemisphere, it marks the shortest day – or the longest night – of the year. The Sun and the North Pole are at their farthest points from each other on this day. It will come as no surprise, then, to learn that the word 'solstice' comes from the Latin, *solstitium* – meaning 'sun stands still'.

Cultures all over the world have their own unique traditions when it comes to the winter solstice, but what unifies them is a profound reverence for natural forces and a communal cheer for the lighter days to come. Embracing and accepting this inevitable occurrence is a healthy step on the road to improving our mental health, particularly if we mark its passing by paying homage to nature. By simply scattering seeds for birds, we are giving back to our wild community. Or we can celebrate the sun and the brighter, lighter days to come with a candle ritual; placing an unlit candle in the centre of a ring of candles, we light each candle, leaving our central 'sun' candle until last. During this ritual, we can focus on gratitude for what we have and for Earth's wondrous natural cycles. We can also take inspiration from seasonal ingredients – such as celeriac, parsnips, squash, fennel and cranberries – and nature's superstar spice: ginger.

SOLSTICE GINGERBREAD

Ginger has been a traditional winter-solstice spice in Europe ever since it was brought over by crusaders around the year 1100. Delicious homemade gingerbread is a wonderful, celebratory treat for any time of the day.

INGREDIENTS FOR TWO DOZEN PORTIONS

- 225 g of self-raising flour, a teaspoon of bicarbonate of soda, 2 tablespoons of ginger and a teaspoon of mixed spice
- 100 g each of diced butter, black treacle, light muscovado sugar and golden syrup
- One free-range egg (beaten) and 275 ml of full fat milk

METHOD

1. Preheat your oven to 180° C or Gas mark 4, then line a 30 x 23 cm baking tray with baking paper.

2. Mix your flour, bicarbonate of soda, mixed spices and ginger in a bowl.

3. Now heat your butter, treacle, syrup and sugar in a saucepan until the butter melts. Leave to cool for a minute or two, then pour into your mixed dry ingredients, add your beaten egg, add your milk and beat the whole mixture with a wooden spoon until it's smooth.

4. Pour into your tin and bake for approximately 35 minutes, or until it's golden brown and springy to the touch.

5. Serve warm with vanilla ice cream. You can freeze any leftovers for up to a week, or wrap tightly in clingfilm and put in a tin for eating within three to four days.

FLOWERS IN ICE

As the last of the winter months approaches, what better way to capture winter's beauty, and pamper yourself with a wonderful sensory treat than to make some stunning, romantic floral ice cubes from the season's edible wildflowers? Pansies, violas, lavender and borage (also know as the 'star flower') are vividly coloured, delicate and utterly gorgeous when crystallised in ice cubes, and they're good for you, too. Add your pretty cubes to a cocktail or a refreshing glass of water, and give yourself a real treat.

You'll need a silicone ice-cube tray (choose one that has larger cube shapes for optimum effect), some edible flowers (like those mentioned above, but do research others that may be more abundant where you live) and, for extra clear ice, use distilled, boiled and then cooled water.

HOW TO MAKE:

1. Gather your flowers, making sure you have permission to pick them if they are not from your garden. Ideally, you'll need a mix of varieties of different colours, and those with smaller, petite petals are ideal.

2. Cut your flower stems, leaving no more than half an inch of each stem.

3. Fill your ice tray with water to a quarter of the depth.

4. Now place your flowers face-down in the water and put the tray in the freezer.

5. When the water has frozen, remove the tray and add more water, this time to half the depth of the tray. Now put the tray back in the freezer.

6. As before, when the water has frozen, remove the tray and fill it right up to the top, then put it back in the freezer.

7. When all the water in your tray has completely frozen, remove the tray and serve your floral ice cubes with a drink – for yourself, your friends or, if you're feeling romantic, your beloved other half.

ORGANISE A WINTER TREASURE HUNT

A fabulous way to motivate yourself and your friends or family to get outside in the winter months is to make it a mission, by organising a nature treasure hunt! This activity, closely associated with childhood, is a wonderfully comforting form of play which combines fun with exercise, sharpens mental agility and, most importantly, gets us out into the crisp winter air.

HOW TO SET IT UP

1. First, choose an area to conduct the treasure hunt. This can be somewhere familiar to you, or somewhere you have thoroughly investigated for all its nooks and crannies. Your local park or woodland might work, or your garden if you have one – and if it's a communal garden, you can invite your neighbours and get to know them better. Just make sure you won't be trespassing.

2. Take a notebook with you for your reccy. Note down each hiding place, focusing on any significant landmarks and the shape of the space. Googling a map of the area when you get home will help you to create your map.

3. Get creative with drawing your map, using coloured pens to indicate grass, flowers and woodland, any notable buildings, benches or statues, then create your clues. This is the fun part where you get to think up riddles that your players have to unpick in order to find the treasure.

4. Now choose your treasure. This can be anything from beads or marbles to natural materials such as winter leaves or clusters of safe berries. Small objects are better. Put these in small plastic containers, then return to your trail and hide them in holes, hang them from branches, or bury them underground.

5. Roll up copies of your map and your clues like a scroll, and hand out to your friends.

6. Check the weather and pick a day for the hunt accordingly. Avoid rain, but a snowy treasure hunt has a truly magical feel to it.

UPDATE
YOUR DÉCOR

Are you looking to add something else to your winter mental-health armoury? Some visual tricks can go a long way towards lifting your mood, and taking inspiration from the natural world keeps your connection to it. Whether it's through the colours and textures in your house or the lock-screen wallpaper on your devices, surrounding yourself with the very best of nature's colours and materials is guaranteed to make you feel more positive.

If you're up for some practical work, painting your walls to reflect nature's colours can transform a room, and your mood along with it. If your living space is small, think about painting or wallpapering just one wall in a room. For a springtime feel, try a pale, leafy green or a sky blue. If you're looking for a summery colour, try a sunny yellow, and for autumnal or wintery vibes, russets and golds are cosy and majestic. The best way to keep your connection to nature during the winter months is to gather natural finds from outside and bring them in to your home. Fallen leaves, cones, wood and wildflowers will infuse a room with the smells and sights of winter. You can leave them as they are, or get creative with spray paint, ribbons and design. Even if your taste is for minimal décor, touches of nature around your home – a trail of ivy over a shelf or mantelpiece, a bowl of sparkling pine cones, or glorious conkers, or an arrangement of seasonal flowers such as bluebells, pansies, violas, cyclamen or hellebores in your kitchen or bedroom – will transform your living space. In a season that often seems the least colourful, winter's natural beauty is there to be found and celebrated, even when you can't get outside as much as you'd like.

ADAPT YOUR ROUTINES

We are creatures of habit, and we can find ourselves stuck in the same old daily rituals and routines, day in, day out, for years. Some of these routines are important and healthy, but some are actually a way of avoiding our feelings. Here are some ideas to help you change up your routine.

1. Make a list of your regular activities — those guaranteed to boost your mood, like reading or cooking, as well as those that may be more like crutches such as drinking alcohol, smoking, staring at your screen or scrolling through social media feeds.

2. Consider how you can cut out or cut down on these crutch habits and have something lined up to replace them – or make more time for things you know make you feel healthy and happy.

3. Don't put pressure on yourself to stop a habit cold turkey, even one you know is not too healthy, as this may exacerbate anxiety and stress.

4. Do reflect on which habits or activities leave you feeling good for a sustained period. Swapping emotional crutches such as endless screen-scrolling for a handful of the activities in this book will do wonders for your emotional wellbeing.

5. Don't forget, you can combine really worthwhile passions, such as reading, with time in nature. Audiobooks and podcasts can keep you connected to stories, news or comedy while you're strolling through the park or across a forest. Simply by breathing in fresh air and walking past trees and flowers or on a path strewn with snow-tipped winter leaves, you are treating yourself to a wellbeing-enhancing experience.

6. Always think about how kind you are being to yourself with any activity. Listen to your body and mind when they tell you something isn't working for you.

NURTURING THE EARTH

One simple way to really feel connected to nature and thus improve our mental wellbeing, is by giving nature a helping hand in winter. If you're lucky enough to have a garden or decent-sized balcony then you can start there. If you don't have any outside space of your own, you can still do your bit in a friend or relative's garden, or your local green space.

A wonderful way to help nature is to make a compost heap. Compost is formed of organic matter, which improves the structure of soil and its capacity to retain water and vital nutrients for plant growth.

MAKING GOOD COMPOST

1. You'll need something to contain your compost (a plastic moulded container with a perforated bottom, or a wooden crate, but do seek expert advice on this if you're not sure). Old pieces of carpet, combined with your compost, will keep in the heat that's made from what's called 'aerobic bacteria', which nicely accelerates the composting process.

2. You'll need two kinds of waste: 'wet' waste such as grass clippings and 'dry' waste such as fallen leaves, dry plant stems, wood shavings or straw. Alternate layers of wet and dry waste.

3. Make sure your compost container is positioned so that it's sheltered from the wind, which will cool its contents down.

4. Rest your container on top of the soil, to allow earthworms to tunnel in and help the composting process. To keep out vermin, put a layer of chicken wire on top of the soil and underneath your container.

5. The composting process can take up to a year, but if your heap is insulated well, and you add in 'compost maker' (you get this from any gardening centre or a credited online source), then it will speed things up considerably.

GIVE NATURE A HELPING HAND

Though it's important not to put food out for wildlife too regularly (they need to be self-reliant), in winter's harshest conditions, a little extra help is important. There are lots of ways to make life easier for wildlife in winter, but here are a few that are easy to implement in your own garden or a friend's.

1. For birds, scatter or put out seeds or food waste, such as berries, or fruit like pears, apples or plums.

2. Hungry hedgehogs appreciate a little dog or cat food (though make sure it isn't fish based) and are partial to the odd boiled and chopped-up egg.

3. Squirrels love hazelnuts and walnuts, but they'll also tuck in to sunflower seeds and tasty carrots, too.

4. For all wildlife, leaving out fresh water is invaluable for hydration, as freezing temperatures can make natural water sources inaccessible.

5. If a pond ices over, break the surface so any pondlife can escape.

6. Empty bird feeders, boxes and baths and clean them with some hot water and mild detergent. This encourages good hygiene in our feathered friends, and keeps them in tip-top condition.

7. Even if you're tempted, leave pruning herbaceous plants (those plants whose flowers die in autumn, but whose roots stay alive all year) until spring. Unpruned, they provide great homes for sheltering insects.

8. Make sure that any netting, such as tennis netting or football netting, is lifted just above the ground so that wildlife doesn't get tangled up or injured in it.

WINTER PHOTOSHOOT

As with all the other seasons, capturing photos of the world outside during winter reminds us not only of its beauty, but of its vital importance to all our lives. The wildlife, flowers and plants, the snow, rain, sun and wind, the tiniest of living things… all are working to keep the planet alive, to provide us with vitamin-rich food and keep our immune systems strong.

But in order to truly feel the gifts that nature gives us, we have to pay attention and show it respect. The goal is to learn to love each season for its unique contribution and embrace the rain along with the sun and the cold with the hot. We want to celebrate nature's incredible evolving palette and incorporate as much of it into our lives as we can.

You can capture photos of winter from its start in November to its easing in late February/early March by creating a winter photo album. Try to get up in time to watch dawn rise; on a clear morning it will blaze a tawny yellow through bare tree silhouettes. Have fun spotting foxes and squirrels, listening to the birds' dawn chorus and marvelling at the patterns made by frost on grass and leaves. Look up at the sky and snap pictures of the changes in its colour, as it turns from crisp and blue to dark and stormy. Create eternal memories of the colours you see during winter, from snowdrops and scarlet berries, to rich-green ivy and brown leaves on the ground. The purpose of your journal is to reflect your emotions as they evolve throughout the season, and to remind you of your own cycle which mirrors that of the natural world.

Snowy adventures filled the pages of the books we read as children, transporting us to magical worlds. But as we move into adulthood, we often lose a little of our awe and excitement. Photographing the natural spaces around us as they are blanketed with snow – where the trees sparkle and icy patterns form on the ground – is a wonderful excuse to get outside and breathe in that frosty air, feeling the exhilaration of being wrapped up warm as our cheeks tingle.

Take a friend with you and capture an afternoon on film. You could also set yourself a creative project: build a mini igloo, or a snow-person. Depending on where you live, snow is not guaranteed to happen every year, so make the most of it when it comes!

SNOWY PHOTOSHOOT TIPS

1. Make sure you have the right clothes and footwear. Thermal layers of man-made fabric are best for your upper half, along with a windproof coat, thermal gloves and a hat. Flexible sports leggings are ideal – avoid denim, which will get wet and stay wet.

2. Footwear is important as slipping and sliding on icy paths can be perilous and you need grip on the soles of your shoes. Hiking trainers have good grip, but walking boots are ideal. Do some research and find the best boots for you.

3. Keep moving if you can. This will get your heart pumping enough to keep you warm.

4. As with sledging, if you have back or joint issues, or suffer with weak bones, avoid icy conditions. Tramping through fresh snow on grass is probably fine, but trying to navigate slippery pavements will be stressful – which is the exact opposite of how you should feel on your snowy photoshoot!